The Aberdyfi Guide

Richard Mayou

y lolfa

Cambriae Typus, Humphrey Llwyd (1527–68).

One of the earliest maps of Wales and the first to show Wales as a separate country (extending into the English Marches). For millennia the Celtic Sea was filled with small boats trading between the many tiny Welsh and Irish harbours. They also sailed to southern (Milford Haven, Tenby, Swansea, Cardiff and especially Bristol) and northern deep-water ports (Conwy, Chester, Liverpool) which traded with English, French and other continental ports.

The Aberdyfi Guide

Richard Mayou

First impression: 2026

Cover image: Glyn Davies
Book design: Fizog Design
ISBN: 978-1-80099-833-9

Published and printed in Wales on paper from well-maintained forests by
Y Lolfa Cyf., Talybont, Ceredigion, SY24 5HE

Web: ylolfa.com
Email: ylolfa@ylolfa.com
Tel: 01970 832 304

y olfa

Contents

Preface

When I was aged ten, my parents bought a decrepit house on an estuary headland two miles upriver from Aberdyfi. Since then, my family and I have walked, swum and explored the area. Above all, we have enjoyed astounding views of the weather, tides and wildlife. Five years ago I published a book about the Dyfi estuary. Now this book continues the story.

It has taken me a lifetime to discover how long the history of Aberdyfi is, and how much evidence of an underappreciated past we can still find on the ground. I have tried to show this in both my text and choice of images. It is not a definitive history. It is an overview which can be read from beginning to end or dipped into. It is also a picture book in which each image and caption complements the main text but can be enjoyed in its own right. There is more to discover and I would welcome corrections and comments at **richard.mayou@nuffield.ox.ac.uk**

For me, it has been an opportunity to meet many people who know and care a great deal about Dyfi life, and its geography and history. My acknowledgements are many and are listed at the end of the book.

The book is dedicated to my brother Bryan and to the memory of my parents and my wife Ann, who all so greatly enjoyed the estuary and our house.

Aran Fawddwy
2,969tr
Craiglyn Dyfi
Gogledd
Dinas Mawddwy
Cerist
Cader Idris 2,930tr
Machynlleth
Abermaw
Tywyn
AFON DYFI
Aberystwyth
BAE CEREDIGION
Pysgod y Dyfi
(Fish of the Dyfi)
Brithyll
(Brown trout)
Brithyll y Môr
(Sea trout)
Eog
(Salmon)
A scale of 7 kilometers
Lledfron
Clywedog
Nant y Dugoed
Tafalog
Carton
Waun Gau
Iain
Twymyn
Ednant
Crugnant
Gwydol
Goedwig
Ffernant
Crewi
Carrog
De Dulas
Ceniarth
Hengwm
Angell
Gogledd Dulas
Ceiriog
Llwydo
Rhonwydd
Alys
Pennal
Llyfnant
Cymerau
Einion
Pemprys
Ddu
Cletwr
Ceulan
Cyneiniog
Leri

Introduction

Estuaries are places where freshwater rivers meet tidal saltwater, resulting in special wildlife habitats and sheltered harbours. They are the sites of most of the world's ports and entrepôts, such as the great deep-water ports of London and Bristol and the ports of south Wales. The Dyfi estuary is much smaller but is still very special:

- Outstanding natural habitats.
- Aberdyfi is the most sheltered and best of the many Cardigan Bay harbours.
- It is the entry to a river navigable to the strategic centre of Wales and surrounded by natural wealth – timber, wool, tanneries, lead, silver, slate.

Aerial view of Aberdyfi, Toby Driver, RCAHMW, 2011.

The now mainly nineteenth-century centre of the village. From the end of the eighteenth century the original waterside settlement extended successively up Chapel Square and Copper Hill Street, east along Seaview Terrace, west along Glandyfi and Bodfor Terraces, and then up Church Street.

(opposite) **The Dyfi with its estuary and tributaries**, drawn by Liz Fenwick.

It rises at 1,900 feet above sea level from Creiglyn Dyfi, a small lake below Aran Fawddwy, and shares watersheds with the rivers Hafren (Severn) and Dyfrdwy (Dee). Other streams enter from the slopes of Pumlumon and from a much smaller northern catchment. The Dyfi is a short (30 miles) and fast-flowing river which floods rapidly with highlands rain, high tides and westerly gales. Like many other estuaries, it reaches the sea via a narrow channel and bar.

Although the village that we know today is largely a nineteenth-century creation, it began long ago as a small area of sheltered estuary shore next to deep water. Inevitably, it became a place for mooring, warehouses, trans-shipping and waiting for tides and winds. Over the centuries it has been, successively, a fishing port, a river ferry, a centre for mining and trade, and a place for visitors, each layer of history leaving its traces in the twenty-first century.

This not just a parochial story. As I described in *The Dyfi Estuary: An Illustrated History*, the Dyfi valley has been a strategic route by water, and then road and railway, for connecting the heart of Wales to the world. Seemingly remote and rural, yet the story of Aberdyfi has a national and occasionally international significance.

This book begins with an account of this background and then describes walks that follow the chronology of an expanding village.

The Dyfi Estuary, Photograph © Glyn Davies

Chapter One

Background

The changing estuary

From 25,000 years ago, the estuary as we know it was formed.

- **AD1300:** Formation of sand dunes begins.
- **1600 onwards:** Manmade changes to the Dyfi river channel: fish traps, embankments, drainage.
- **1800s:** Large-scale land drainage at Borth and Tywyn.
- **1827:** A turnpike road along the Dyfi shore provides easy land access to Aberdyfi and enables new building along the waterside.
- **Mid 1860s:** The railway supersedes coastal trade, alters the estuary flow and brings new prosperity, including many more visitors.
- **Twentieth and twenty-first centuries:** Climate change and agricultural pollution continue to alter the Dyfi and increase flooding. Much new building at Aberdyfi around the historic centre of the village.

(opposite) **Artist's sketch map of Aberdyfi at the end of the eighteenth century as the geographically inevitable place for mooring and transshipping**, drawn by Liz Fenwick.

A narrow and shallow entrance from the sea leads to deep water opposite a confined waterside area with warehouses, ferry station and several houses. Workers' cottages are being erected at the bottom of a valley in Chapel Square and the new Copper Hill Street. There are newly-dug copper and lead mines above the village. A leat (watercourse) from a reservoir high up at Y Horon supplies a water wheel on Balkan Hill.

A narrow track below a steep and winding shoreline connects Aberdyfi to an inlet, valley and stream at Penhelyg. Higher up there are hillside tracks and a number of sixteenth-century and later farmhouses surrounded by fields whose names are still in use today. The main land access is from the present Church Street (and perhaps also Copper Hill Street) over the hill to Dyffryn Gwyn in Cwm Maethlon (Happy Valley). Another farm track, eventually known as Ffordd Top (top road), led along the crest of the hills past Carn Mach Arthur to Pennal.

To the west there is a common land marsh behind the sand dunes, with place-names which refer to marsh or water. Tywyn is reached either over the sand at low tide or by a track between the marsh and higher ground. To the south of the estuary is the ferry low-tide landing stage at Craig y Penrhyn.

The underlying rocks around the Dyfi are very old, laid down between *c.*440 and *c.*420 million years ago, but the landscape we see today is very new. About 25,000 years ago, massive glaciers on Pumlumon began to retreat and their meltwater carved out a deep channel 130 feet below today's sea level. By the end of the Ice Age, around 9500BC, the land surface covered by forest extended far to the west of the present coastline. Then, as the climate warmed, the sea level rose dramatically and, by around 4000BC, all was swallowed by the sea. As the seashore retreated it left behind tree stumps, still occasionally uncovered by storms, and three submerged reefs (sarnau) extending into Cardigan Bay: Sarn Cynfelin, just south of Wallog, between Borth and Clarach; Sarn y Bwlch, near Tywyn; and Sarn Badrig (St Patrick's Causeway), just south of Harlech. This is the real story of the fabled submerged land of Cantre'r Gwaelod.

Cantre'r Gwaelod and 'The Bells of Aberdovey'

The flooding of Cardigan Bay has led to legends about the lost low-lying sixth-century kingdom of Cantre'r Gwaelod (The Lowland Hundred). The many versions agree that it was surrounded by a dyke, with sluice gates which had to be closed as the tide came in. One day, the custodian of the dyke, Seithenyn, a notorious drunkard, left the gates open and the sea came in, submerging the kingdom. The fossilised tree stumps and the undersea reefs or sarnau were claimed to be remains of the forests and of the dams which protected Cantre'r Gwaelod. Since then, it is said, the bells of the churches under the sea toll to call the people back.

St Peter's Church, Aberdyfi, did not originally have bells, but now has a carillon which plays tunes and hymns. These include 'The Bells of Aberdovey', a much loved song from **Charles Dibdin**'s English comic opera, *Liberty Hall*, of 1785. The first Welsh translation (Clychau Aberdyfi) was, perhaps, performed in 1838. The best-known version of the words is:

If to me you can be true,
Just as true as I to you,
It's one, two, three, four, five and six
Sing the Bells of Aberdovey.
One, two, three, four, five and six
It's one, two, three, four, five and six
Sing the bells of Aberdovey.

Aberdyfi began on a small area of waterside flat land at the foot of a valley with steep hills sloping to the estuary to the east and marsh and sand dunes to the west. A narrow, winding track led to a smaller valley at Penhelyg. Until the nineteenth century, the main access was by water. Ships under sail had a hazardous passage at sea, as evidenced by the many wrecks, and then a tricky entry into the harbour. There were unpredictable winds and tides, a changeable channel and, at its mouth, a narrow bar formed by nearly parallel banks of sand. Once reached, Aberdyfi was a safe harbour with a deep pool for moorings, and places where ships could be beached for loading and unloading, provisioning, and for repair. Boats would then either travel upriver to the tidal limit close to Machynlleth, or trans-ship goods were carried by smaller river boats. Leaving Aberdyfi harbour against the prevailing south-westerly wind was also difficult, and boats often had to wait days for a favourable wind and tide.

Over the centuries, the course of the Dyfi and its estuary have been greatly changed by natural causes and manmade events, such as land drainage, the cutting out of meanders, building fish traps and railway embankments. These changes are continuing and the

(opposite) **The mouth of the estuary with the sand bar: A view from a microlight**, © Glyn Davies.

Aberdyfi fromYnyslas, © Glyn Davies.

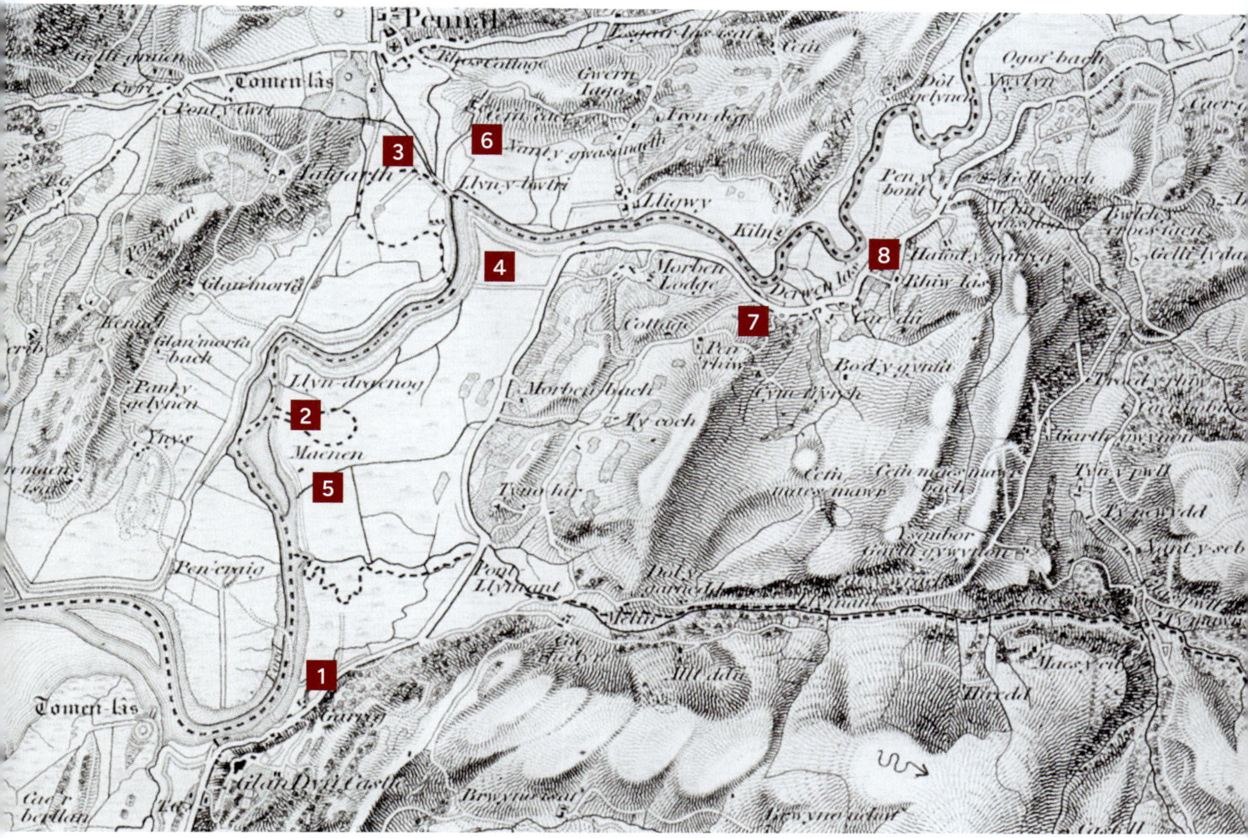

Ordnance Survey Map, 1 inch, First Edition, 1837, showing river features.

The river has always had a complicated and varying channel, with a succession of deep-water pools. Most imports and exports were taken to or from landing stages at Garreg (now Glandyfi) and Derwenlas. Crews often had to row their boats or pull them by lines to kedge anchors to the shore. Boats frequently moored between tides in one of the river pools, such as Llyn-y-Draenog (hedgehog pool) and Llyn Bwtri (buttery pool) near Pennal.

1 Garreg: It was the main wharf for sixteenth- and seventeenth-century silver, lead and lead ore. It was, and remains, a base for fishermen netting salmon.

2 Llyn-y-Draenog: A deep-water mooring, named after a device used for dredging the channel.

3 Pennal Wharf and Tramway, from Cwm Ebol slate quarry.

4 Llyn Bwtri: A noted whirlpool (like churning butter) when the tide was high. It became a pool where ships could remain afloat when the tide dropped. There were wharfs and shipbuilding on its shore.

5 Maenan farmhouse: It was also a tavern for sailors passing, and moored boats. The ruins of a rectangular stone building are still visible.

6 Cefn Caer: The site of the Roman fort which had access to a river landing stage and a ford or a ferry.

7 Morben (the end of the sea): A site for shipbuilding and Cei Ward Wharf. Probable site of a ford and a ferry.

8 Derwenlas: The main river port from the eighteenth century, with wharfs for slate and other cargoes, and shipbuilding.

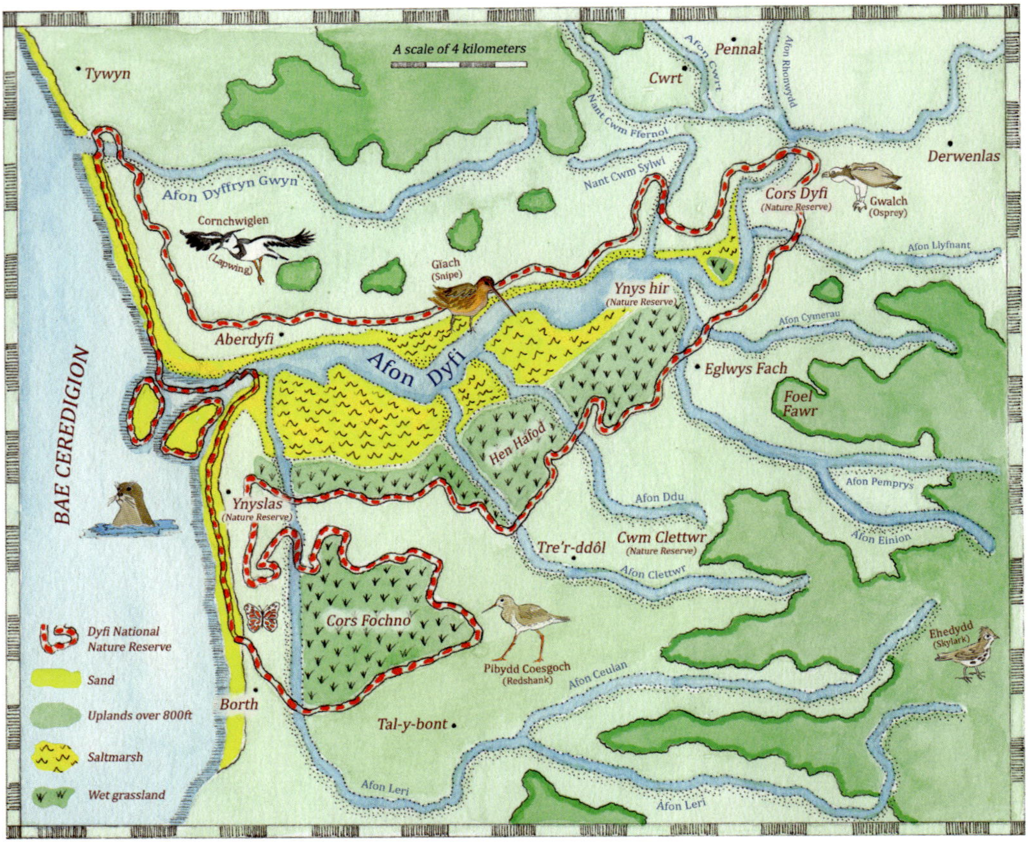

The principal Dyfi habitats and the Dyfi National Nature Reserve, drawn by Liz Fenwick.

Heroic efforts by conservation charities, such as the RSPB and the Montgomeryshire Wildlife Trust, and others, have established nationally important accessible reserves on the southern shore of the Dyfi – RSPB Ynys-Hir, Dyfi Wildlife Centre, Cwm Clettwr, Cors Fochno (Borth bog) and Ynyslas.

river has become less navigable in my lifetime. Sediment continues to slowly silt the estuary, agricultural and other pollution is a problem, and the areas of Spartina grass are expanding. The greatest threat is climate change, with rising temperatures and sea levels altering ecology and causing more frequent and severe flooding.

The weather is also changing but it is a complicated story. The climate has varied over the millennia since the last Ice Age, affecting agriculture and daily life. There was a Medieval Warm Period from 950 to 1100, and a Little Ice Age in the seventeenth century. Aberdyfi now has a maritime climate – mild, but sometimes cloudy, wet and windy – and our local sunshine, rainfall and wind exposure are affected by the shapes of the coastline and the hills. The seashore is exposed to south-westerly winds with fierce winter gales, while the mountains force moist air to rise very quickly, resulting in considerably more rain inland. However, the coast at Aberdyfi has some of the mildest and sunniest weather in

A microlight view of Aberdyfi from the south, © Glyn Davies.

A surprisingly green village where open spaces and large gardens are surrounded by hillside and the estuary.

Wales throughout the year. The late Sir John Houghton (1931–2020), a most distinguished Welsh physicist and meteorologist, was so impressed by what he identified as Aberdyfi's microclimate, that he chose it for his retirement home.

Recent climate change has already given us hotter, drier summers, and warmer, wetter winters, which have altered land and water temperatures, weather patterns and the sea level. There have been larger and more frequent floods and it is already clear that the beach defences and peat and railway embankments are inadequate. The seashore, much of Borth, and the estuary habitats are all threatened. Winter storms increasingly wash sand on the Aberdyfi waterfront and fill cellars with seawater.

Natural history

Over recent centuries, the natural history of the Dyfi and its shores has become degraded, but in the last 60 years the estuary has become the centre of the most designated habitats in Wales, with nationally distinguished reserves. Aberdyfi village is surrounded by varied habitats and is a surprisingly rewarding place to find many species of mammals, fish, birds and plants.

The Dyfi area has attracted naturalists since the time of Edward Llwyd (1660–1709), one of the greatest Welsh antiquaries, naturalists and scholars of his time. Many of his plant specimens, some from Aberdyfi, survive in the Oxford University Herbaria. More recently, Birmingham-born William (Bill) Condry (1918–98) remains the most significant Dyfi naturalist, a considerable ornithologist, botanist and ecologist who worked tirelessly for the landscape as a successful wildlife author and powerful advocate. In 1950, he and his wife Penny, a most capable botanist, lived briefly at Glygyrog Ddu, high above Aberdyfi, before moving across the estuary and leading the founding of RSPB Ynys-Hir. Their work and the efforts of others has resulted in the village being located on the most designated estuary in Wales: including the UNESCO Biosphere Reserve, European recognition as a Special Protection Area for rare birds, and a larger Special Area of Conservation which takes account of marine and estuarine wildlife. There are two British National Nature

Aberdyfi Birds

Apart from the common garden birds, year-round birds include:

- Jackdaws – a flock giving acrobatic displays in strong winds.
- Herring gulls have declined, to be 'Birds of Conservation Concern'. They have added human food remains to their diminishing natural sea food and learnt to drop mussels on hard surfaces. They have also moved from cliff habitats to village chimneys and roofs.
- Tawny owls, which are especially vocal from December to February at the beginning of their breeding season, to be found around the Edwardian trees on Balkan Hill.
- Crows.
- Rooks with rookeries in tall trees in Penhelyg and Mynydd Isaf.
- Shell ducks which nest in trees before taking their ducklings to sea.
- Goosanders, shags and cormorants fishing in the estuary.
- Wood pigeons and collared doves.
- Buzzards and red kites over the hillsides.
- Grey herons, which have added nocturnal fishing by the light of street lamps along the waterfront.

Spring and summer visitors include ospreys, egrets and several species of warblers on the bank which drops from Rhoslan to Morfa Gipsies.

Winter rarities include a small flock of Greenland Lesser White-fronted geese and another of pintail ducks, as well as other spring and autumn migrants.

Reserves (Cors Fochno and Ynyslas) on the other side of the estuary, and there are Welsh Sites of Special Scientific Interest, especially for plants, within the village.

Recent changes in land use and farming, pollution and climate change, have resulted in a nationwide loss of habitats, their connectedness and quality causing a reduction in species and their numbers. Although this is true for the Dyfi, its variety of habitats provide niches for special species and some wonderful encounters with animals and plants.

At sea, plant and animal life is particularly rich around the three sarnau (subtidal reefs), with a great diversity of seaweeds, crustaceans, jellyfish and sea anemones. They support pollock, bass, black bream and grey mullet, which in turn are prey for bottlenose dolphins, porpoises and grey seals, and rarities such as leatherback sea turtles, together with a great variety of seabirds. However, the great autumn shoals of herring that were the basis of Aberdyfi's historic prosperity are no more.

The estuary waters are rich in microscopic plankton animal life which provides food for fish and birds, while the sands house rich populations of invertebrates, including shellfish such as edible cockles, mussels and clams and the more sinister Portuguese man o' war jellyfish. Sadly, there have been catastrophic declines in the previously abundant salmon and sewin (sea trout), but there are still mullet and sea bass. There is a sea bass 'nursery', where fishing is prohibited for part of the summer. Around the harbour warning notices announce that self-concealing weaver fish hide in the sand.

Along the seashore, sand dunes demonstrate the succession of dune formation and growth – from sandy shore through unstable embryo dunes, yellow dunes stabilised by marram grass, and finally to relatively fixed grey dunes and scrub. They are home to rich populations of orchids, mosses, liverworts, fungi, insects and spiders – many of them rare and some unknown elsewhere in Britain. Sand lizards (the males a vivid green) can be seen. In between the grey dunes are dune slacks – low-lying areas that flood readily and have a different flora, including increasingly abundant orchids.

Above the sandy estuary there is a transition to mudflats and salt marshes, which have been built up by natural silting and colonising plants (most conspicuously, cord grass, Spartina). Marine worms and shellfish make this one of Cardigan Bay's most important areas for birdlife. Across the estuary, Cors Fochno (Borth bog) is a very rare example of a raised bog which supports many rare species, including mosses, liverworts and an outstanding range of invertebrates.

Higher up, remnants of ancient semi-natural woodland, predominantly sessile oak, are still present in fragmented areas, including Penhelyg, often with an understorey, or shrub layer, of hawthorn, hazel and blackthorn, with more open areas dominated by bracken and gorse. Large forests of commercial conifer species, planted by the Forestry Commission (now Natural Resources Wales) in the last hundred years, now cover a quarter of the Dyfi catchment and can be seen from the estuary road. The older uniform monoculture blocks of trees, mainly North American Sitka spruce, ruthlessly obliterated bio-diversity. However, since the 1970s, planting has been planned more ecologically, with a much greater range of more attractive and productive species.

Above is ffridd, the characteristic steep upland fringe between the intensively managed lower fields and the uplands. It is enclosed and grazed, with scattered trees, bracken, heather and bilberry heath, grassland, bog and rock.

Higher still are the uplands dominated by a complex mosaic of heathland and bog. Acid rain and over-grazing by sheep has degraded the grasslands, and bracken has become invasive. Even so, heath with heather, bilberry and gorse can be seen around Llyn Barfog (beared lake). Future management to reduce over-grazing and restore the traditional Welsh landscape remains highly controversial.

In spite of the numbers of people and dogs, the village is a surprisingly good place for wildlife. Particularly good spots for observing wildlife are the Penhelyg garden / Roman road area where the Dyfi hits the rocks, the less used part of the beach and sand dunes halfway to Tywyn, and Llyn Barfog, where otters hunt for frogs in early spring. The community council policy of acquiring and protecting less disturbed pieces of habitat has meant that many species not normally found close to housing have found refuge, especially mammals, most of which have become nocturnal. This is confirmed by records of roadkill: otters, badgers, polecats and badgers. More than five types of bat hunt over the village, for example in the Gas Works Reserve, and in the blackthorn around the Pen y Bryn lookout.

Building materials and styles

The oldest buildings are simple in design and use local materials.

- The construction of the turnpike road and of the railway brought new materials and designs to the centre of the village, together with expansion along the waterfront.
- Sales by the Ynys y Maengwyn estate in the 1870s and developing tourism resulted in large houses in varied styles on Balkan Hill, and further development along the waterfront to east and west.
- In the second half of the twentieth century, developers and builders bought land for larger-scale lower-cost developments to the north and west.

(opposite) **Building Features**

1 Local schist stone with residual limewash in the entry to Evans Terrace.

2 Garden walls in Hopeland Avenue.

3 Numbers 13 and 14 Glandyfi Terrace, early nineteenth century with curved bay windows and elegant entrances. Later shopfronts and recent dormer window.

4 Early nineteenth-century houses in New Street with incised render and sash windows. There are ornamented architraves and quoins (render simulating masonry blocks).

5 Numbers 19 and 20 Seaview Terrace rendered with curved bays, original sashes, fine railings and elegant entrances.

6 Brynawel, 26 Seaview Terrace, early nineteeth-century stone, with later ground floor bay windows and roughcast. Particularly fine railings and entrance door.

7 Medical Hall, 18 Glandyfi Terrace, early nineteenth century with fine 1863 shopfront.

1

2

3

4

5

6

7

Aberdyfi's architecture reflects village history. Though few of the earliest buildings survive, from the late eighteenth century right through to the late twentieth, the village's buildings clearly chart its development from port and industrial settlement to holiday resort. In style and materials, they present a charming mix of local and national influences, including Georgian classical, Victorian Gothic, and Arts and Crafts, interpreted by local architects, builders and craftsmen, and mostly using local materials until the railway made it easier to import a greater variety.

Building materials

The locally-dug building stone consists of thin schist slabs, a medium-grained local stone, allied to slate, easily split into thin flakes or plates. Because of its poor quality, few buildings were of exposed stone. Limewash was the traditional protection, supplanted by renders in the early to mid nineteenth century, and by roughcast in the late nineteenth and early twentieth centuries.

Render had its own decorative vocabulary, including the practices of lining out, quoins at external angles, and decorative cornices and architraves. A number of smaller houses are painted (originally limewashed) over the stone, revealing thin narrow ridges of stone underneath. Exceptionally, St Peter's Church and the former Congregational chapel and several houses are of unrendered imported stone. However, even when stone became more available due to the railway, it never supplanted render.

The completion of the railway meant a much wider range of materials became available from the 1860s – brick, roofing materials, standard patterns of doors and windows. While post-railway brick is not uncommon, it is usually only exposed on chimney stacks, and elsewhere tends to be rendered or sometimes painted over, as with Bethel Chapel and Liverpool House. In contrast, the railway station is of bright redbrick with dark blue banding.

Roof coverings: Many of the earliest buildings were originally thatched, but later roofs were of thin slates. After the arrival of the railway, red ridge tiles became common, often in conjunction with redbrick chimneys, particularly so along Glandyfi and Seaview Terraces.

Windows: Sashes were usual. The glazing patterns reflect their date, with older windows having more and smaller panes, thicker glazing bars and lacking the horns (the little supports on the bottom of the upper sashes). Some of the early glazing bars are quite fine and show a relationship between the quality of detail and the status of the house. While the majority have been replaced, some original vertical sash windows remain, for example at 14 and 15 Glandyfi Terrace and several houses on Seaview Terrace and in New Street. Horizontal sliding sash windows survive on Evans Terrace.

The early nineteenth-century houses generally have no bay or dormer windows, though the delicate curved bow windows of 14 and 15 Glandyfi Terrace and 19 and 20 Seaview Terrace show the origins of what later became ubiquitous. As the century progressed so the polygonal, or splayed, bay window came to dominate, both in newly-built houses and in alterations to older buildings. There seems to be an association between the increasing use of

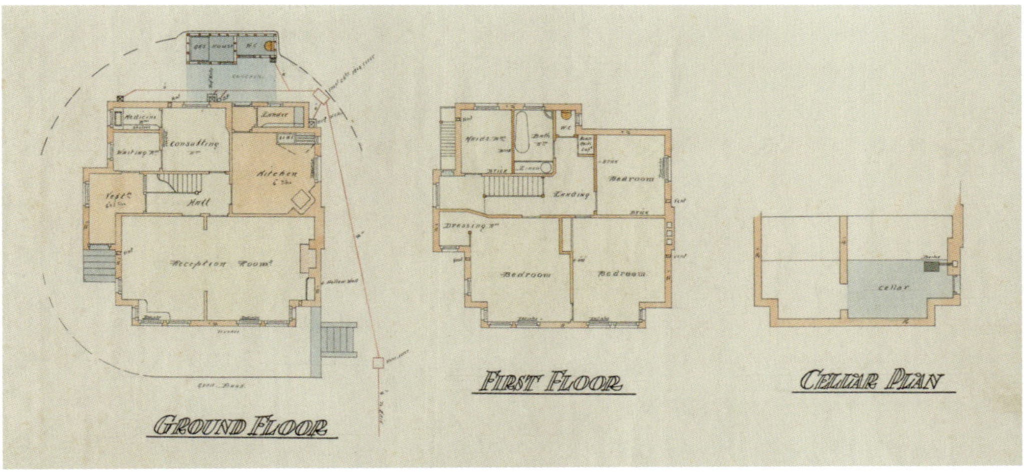

Plan and front elevation for Monkshill, Aberdyfi, 1913. Architect: Charles F. Ellis. A house and 0.8 acres in Corbett Lane designed for Dr F.S. Jackson as a home and consulting room.

Charles F. Ellis (1877–1946) had a large influence on the village between the wars and on what we see today. Born in Barmouth, the son of a builder, he lived most of his life at Maybank on Penhelyg Road, which had been built by his father. After being apprenticed to a local architect, he began a practice at Maybank in 1901. He designed or built 60 buildings in Aberdyfi, including Philip Avenue, Penhelyg Terrace, houses around Gwelfor Road and alterations to Bethel Chapel. He also built local cottage hospitals and supervised Machynlleth Garden Village. He was a jovial and popular man who knew about building on steep hillsides and working with local tradesmen. His very considerable archive was rescued and organised by a nephew after his widow's death, and was the subject of a touring exhibition in 1975. He is an interesting example of an obscure, moderately talented architect who, in an area without great architectural expectations, had a considerable but largely forgotten local impact. Though most of the houses he designed are much altered, some have great charm.

bays and the rise of Aberdyfi as a resort. Similarly, dormer windows became widely popular.

Doorways: There are a good number of examples of classically inspired doorways, combining columns or fluted pilasters with cornices and panelled doors. Many of the doorways on Glandyfi Terrace and on New Street are round arched. From the mid nineteenth century there are examples similar to houses in Aberystwyth, with raised architraves around doors and windows, sometimes picked out in different colours.

Shop fronts: From the later nineteenth century there are numerous well-crafted new shop fronts. Particularly good early examples can be seen at 13a, 14 and 15 Glandyfi Terrace and most dramatically at Medical Hall.

Building styles

The earliest buildings to survive are the scattered sixteenth- and seventeenth-century farmhouses on the hillsides, such as Rhowniar's Cruck Hall, Trefri Fawr and Tafolgraig. Within the village there are simple stone eighteenth- and early nineteenth-century workers cottages.

Following the building of the turnpike, a number of handsome houses were built on Seaview Terrace to the east of the new church. Then came rendered houses and terraces in the Georgian tradition for mariners. They were mainly plain until elements of Gothic were cautiously introduced in the nineteenth century, and later waterfront terraces of lodging houses in styles similar to those at other seaside towns and villages. Some houses still have the names of ships built in the village – such as Mervinia, Maglona and Xanthus, while shops proclaimed their trade connections – London House, Liverpool House.

From the end of the nineteenth century large, and some particularly charming smaller, detached houses spread up the hillside in a variety of Victorian and Arts and Crafts styles. Most had large gardens and impressive views. The most prolific architect was locally-based Charles F. Ellis. Several houses were designed by nationally distinguished architects such as Oswald Milne (Rhowniar) and Clough Williams-Ellis (Brynawelon) and others are unknown or by local builders (Maybank).

In the twentieth century there was increasing diversity of new building, including low-cost estates. Older buildings were modified with extra storeys, bay windows, large dormers and new façades and shop fronts. Traditionally a grey and white limewash village, Aberdyfi has recently become multi-coloured, with many buildings painted in cheerful colours. There have been some developments that are very characteristic of their period, such as Mynydd Isaf and Hillside Village. However, it is disappointing that, despite much use of glass and other modernist features, there has been no architecturally outstanding building since the Second World War.

Gardens

A number of older houses have large and well planted gardens which can be glimpsed from the roads. They benefit from the microclimate and include Plas Trefri, Coed y Glyn, Plas Penhelig, the now separate garden behind Penhelig Lodge, and the houses of Hopeland Road.

Conservation

Since the Second World War there have been administrative attempts to preserve the most architecturally significant buildings and also the general character of the village. There is one Grade II*-listed building (Rhowniar's Cruck Hall) and 32 Grade II-listed buildings and a conservation area for the heart of the village and Penhelyg. However, despite the considerable powers these give to the local authority and the Snowdonia National Park, they have not been notably successful. Inappropriate plastic and misshapen windows, roofing, insensitive additions, inappropriate render, and removal of architectural detail are all frequent. Regrettably, proposals to increase listings and expand the conservation area have not been pursued. Even more regrettably, current powers are not being used.

Chapter Two

A History of Aberdyfi

Origins

It all began long before written records, with extensive Welsh coastal trade connecting with major British ports and with the rest of Europe as shown by the many finds around the estuary of Bronze Age, Iron Age and Roman pottery, tools and ancient mining. There is vestigial evidence of Bronze Age mining nearby at Panteidal and Corbet Dovey. There are substantial remains of Iron Age hill forts to the north and south.

Meirionnydd was the last part of Wales to be conquered by the Romans in AD79. They built roads, a fort and ford at Pennal, a smaller fort opposite Aberdyfi at Erglodd, and they mined metals. Their shipping and armies became frequent sights in and around the Dyfi for over 300 years.

There are few documented facts about the 600 years between the end of Roman rule at the end of the fourth century and the coming of the Normans. The Dyfi was a frontier, a crossing and a meeting point. Aberdyfi harbour must have been involved in the now baffling internecine internal strife which ended with the dominance of Gwynedd. It is said that Maelgwn, king of Gwynedd during the early sixth century, was recognised as pre-eminent among the Welsh kings in a ceremony on the sands of the estuary, which is now called Traeth Maelgwyn.

There were also raids all around and invasions by outsiders. At first, it was the Irish who repeatedly attacked and settled along the coast. Then, in the ninth and tenth centuries, Viking raiders repeatedly ravaged the coast; they sacked Tywyn in 963 and Llanbadarn Fawr (now on the outskirts of Aberystwyth) in 987.

Amid all the violence, it was also a time of trading, cultural and religious links around the Irish Sea and beyond to the Bay of Biscay. A Welsh Church developed from Roman Christianity in the fifth and sixth centuries. Much the most important local centre was the great monastic or clas church of St Cadfan's at Tywyn.

And then, from the late eleventh century, it took the Normans 200 years to conquer northern Wales. They began with brief forays from the east and south and ended with Edward I's campaigns of 1277 and 1284. The king and his armies travelled frequently on land and sea between his castles at Aberystwyth and Castell y Bere (captured from Llywelyn ap Gruffudd) and would have known the Dyfi.

Historical Timeline

Origins	• Archaeological evidence of Bronze, Iron Age and Roman settlements and trade. • An early medieval period of warring Welsh princes, a Welsh Church and incursions by Irish, Vikings and Anglo Saxons. • From eleventh century, Norman invasions; conquest by Edward I in 1277 and 1284.
Sixteenth and seventeenth century	• Livestock farming flourished, with cattle taken to English markets and sheep used by a cottage-based wool industry and for tanning. • The centre of Cardigan Bay herring fishing. • The principal port for north Ceredigion lead and other exports in the late sixteenth century.
Eighteenth century	• Continuing growth of Dyfi industries. • Aberdyfi port is increasingly busy with coastal and river trade. • Copper and lead mining in Aberdyfi.
Nineteenth-century heyday	• Agricultural revolution until *c.*1870. • Lead and other metal mining and development of the slate trade. • Transport revolutions: sea trade, shipbuilding, new roads, railway. • Cultural revolutions – Nonconformism, the Welsh language, new local government. • The beginning of tourism with lodging houses.
From industry to tourism	• A new Aberdyfi wharf and railway sidings. • River trade collapses and sailing ships are replaced by steamers. • Metal mining and slate quarrying unable to compete with foreign competition. • Agricultural depression and sale of large gentry estates after 1870. • Aberdyfi prospers and expands with new residents and tourism.
Early twentieth century	• The end of coastal shipping. • Increasingly busy tourism and house building. • The 1914–18 war. • Local government responsible for public services.
The Second World War to the present day	• 1939: Building beach and inland defences. • 1943: Preparation for the invasion of France. • 1945: Secret rocket research at Ynyslas. • Post-war expansion of the village for second homes and houses for letting.

Aberdyfi, like the many other smaller harbours, was rudimentary, and ships grounded next to the shore on an ebb tide so that packhorses could come alongside. From the twelfth century, the wealthy imported necessities and luxury goods such as coal, food and wine. The earliest written reference to shipping on the estuary, and probably to any Cardigan Bay trade, is from 1109 when a chronicler noted that: 'Cadwgan and Owen fled into a ship that was lying in the River Dove which had come from Ireland a little while before with exchange in her.'

The first mention of the Dyfi ferry is by Giraldus Cambrensis, Archdeacon of Brecon, who described Meirionnydd as 'the roughst and most dreadful territory in Wales'. On 7 April 1188, when recruiting for the Third Crusade with Archbishop Baldwin, he wrote: 'We crossed the river in boats and so left the diocese of St Davids. Now we were in Merioneth, the territory of the sons of Cynan, the first province of Gwynedd to those coming from that direction and part of the diocese of Bangor. Several of the party, including the Bishop of St Davids, turned back rather than enter the lands of the Princes of Gwynedd.'

There are numerous other references to its shipping. We know Owain Glyndŵr and his army crossed the river. In the late fifteenth century, the poet Dafydd Llwyd of Mathafarn, near Machynlleth, wrote of the pleasures of drinking claret brought upriver. About the same time, the Ceredigion poet Deio ab Ieuan Du wrote to a friend to congratulate him on escaping from the wreck of a ship carrying wine from France. It sank where the Dyfi met the sea, and eight of the ten people on board drowned.

Even though Aberdyfi was no more than a tiny sheltered mooring and river ferry, it was important enough to be marked on the fourteenth-century Gough Map, perhaps the earliest map to show Britain in a geographically recognizable form. The most powerful authority was the Ynys y Maengwyn estate, with its great house on the Tywyn to Bryncrug road.

Sixteenth and seventeenth centuries: a fishing and trading port

In the seventeenth century the estuary and its shores got much busier. Ever larger herds of cattle were driven via Machynlleth to English markets by drovers. Cottages and farms were at the centre of a Meirionnydd wool industry, which sent wool and cloth on packhorses to Shrewsbury. Many of the field names and farmhouses on the hillsides and in Cwm Maethlon survive.

Aberdyfi's first great period of prosperity was as the centre of Cardigan Bay's autumn herring fishing. A survey in 1565 described: 'a Haven and having no habitacion, but only three houses whereunto there is no resorte: save only in the type of herring fishing at which time of fishing there is a wonderfull greate resorte of ffyshers assembled from all places within this Realme with Shippes Boottes and Vessells; and there is one chosen among themselves to be their Admiral.'

The boats fished from the Borth beaches, with the fish distributed locally or preserved in salt for export. In 1649, a famine year, herring were lifesaving in mid Wales. An ambitious plan by an aristocratic London company for salt production in the estuary came to nothing.

Plas Ynys y Maengwyn, near Bryncrug, aquatint, J. Baker and T. Bluck, 1795.

The Ynys y Maengwyn estate of eventually around 8,000 acres extended from Tywyn to Aberdyfi and Pennal. It belonged by complicated descent to the same family from the thirteenth to the nineteenth centuries. The Dyfi ferry was rented from the Crown in the medieval period. Not only landlords of the harbour and ferry, they were considerable patrons of poets, and later of the pioneer of British landscape painting, Richard Wilson, Penegoes, near Machynlleth.

Anne Owen, neé Corbet (1684–1741), and her husband Athelstan Owen, of Llanbrynmair, rebuilt the Plas in the early eighteenth century to replace an earlier mansion burnt to the ground during the civil war by its owner to prevent it from falling into the hands of the parliamentarians. They are commemorated on wall plaques on Copper Hill Street and on the Dovey Hotel. In 1951 the successor Corbett owners (no relation to the Corbet family) gave the Plas to Tywyn Council, who, sadly, neglected and then demolished the grand house and replaced it with a caravan park.

Even though it had no sea-going shipping of its own, Aberdyfi became a leading port in Cardigan Bay. Timber, charcoal for smelting, and oak bark for tanning, were taken on packhorses to landing stages at Garreg (Glandyfi), and exported via Aberdyfi. While much of the trade was local, some ships sailed to Liverpool, Chester, Bristol and London, as well as to Ireland and Europe. From 1559, port officials completed Port Books with details of vessels, cargoes, masters and merchants. The principal imports were grain, coal, timber and lime, and luxuries such as wine, tea and sugar. The main exports were fish, timber, oak bark (sent mainly to Irish ports), hides and leather goods, and farm produce.

From around 1620, in an early prefiguring of the Industrial Revolution, lead ore and metal were exported from new north Ceredigion mines via nearby Garreg. By 1693, William Waller, Captain of the Mines for the Gogerddan estate, wrote that by using river boats to take ingots and ore to the 'big storehouse' at Aberdyfi, it was possible to export 15,000 tons of lead ore, or 10,000 tons of lead, to the value of £90,000 annually.

The Aberdyfi shore became an important entrepôt where ships moored, cargoes were stored and trans-shipped to larger seagoing vessel. It was the beginnings of a village. There were the Raven Inn, a ferry house, lime kilns, Customs, as well as warehouses, as described

Dyfi arts

The Ynys y Maengwyn estate was a considerable patron of the arts.
Two particularly distinguished poets had local connections:

Dafydd ap Gwilym (*c.*1315 – *c.*1350), who was probably born near modern-day Bow Street, was among the greatest poets of Europe in the Middle Ages. He composed *Y Don ar Afon Dyfi* (The Wave on the River Dyfi) when unable to cross the river to reach his adored Morfudd in Llanbadarn Fawr. A translation by Gwyn Thomas (1978) reads:

Happy curly-headed, shrill-voiced Wave,
Don't you stop me (lucky omen) from crossing
To that land there, where I shall be rewarded,
Don't detain me do not hinder.
Solicitous water, for the grace of God
(Who is King-Protector), let me over the Dyfi
Turn back, home of three hundred nets
(I am your poet), you are up there above the water.
Don't keep me from Morfudd, my golden maid.

Ieuan Dyfi, who flourished about 1490, is said to have hailed from Aberdyfi.
He wrote a highly popular *cywydd* (a form of Welsh verse) about how women had been false through all the ages. **Gwerful Mechain**, from nearby in Powys, a famed erotic poet and feminist before her time, wrote an equally popular caustic reply.

The *Bear of Amsterdam*

On 26 October 1597, the 120-ton caravel, *Bear of Amsterdam*, weighed anchor in the Dyfi, probably to acquire stores. She was a survivor of the third Spanish Armada and had missed the hoped-for safety at Milford Haven. Westerly winds stranded the ship, while the Ceredigion and Meirionnydd militia, with their Lord Lieutenants, the Vice-Admiral, and the Justices of the Peace, assembled on the banks of the Dyfi and prepared themselves for a fight – but had neither boats nor cannons. When the ship landed men ashore to seek provisions, the Meirionnydd militia ambushed them, killing two Spaniards and capturing four.

Muskets then had some impact, killing three and wounding others on board before the ship moved out of range during the night. A plan by the Meirionnydd militia to build wooden fire rafts and float them down the river on an outgoing tide failed when the wind turned. The *Bear of Amsterdam* was then able to leave after ten days without further incident, only to surrender later at Dartmouth, devoid of ammunition and short of food.

in the 1677 will of William Vaughan: 'All that messuage houses and garden messuage houses storehouses and gardens in Aberdyfi … and my great storehouse called Tŷ Llwyd, the lime kill and lime storehouse … and all my other storehouse rights, priviledges, profits and inheritances lying between the brookes of Penhelig and Aberdyfi.'

Eighteenth century: the village expands

Britain changed dramatically during the eighteenth century, with revolutions in communication, agriculture, industry and trade. Welsh coastal trade expanded, with around 60 ports and cargo-handling creeks between Chepstow in the south to Chester in the north. Aberdyfi was one of the more important smaller ports and, for a period before 1770, it had a Customs House with three staff. There were many shipwrecks, including around the Dyfi bar, which helped to stimulate map-making of the Welsh coast by Lewis Morris and Murdoch Mackenzie.

Industries prospered around the estuary and river shores. Tanning and leather trades continued to be major employers in Machynlleth, and from the middle of the century the cloth trade was boosted by orders from the plantations of the United States and West Indies. However, there was a pause in lead mining. In 1748, Lewis Morris observed that, 'Here, and at Borth, they have some years a good Herring-fishery, and of other Fish a constant Plenty. But their chief Commodities are Timber and Oak Bark. When the Smelting-houses at Garreg, and the Silver Mills were up, this place was noted for the Lead Trade.'

Towards the end of the century production by north Ceredigion and west Montgomeryshire lead mines recovered, and packhorses and sleds took their ore to ships and river boats at Garreg and Derwenlas. There were also copper and lead mines in the

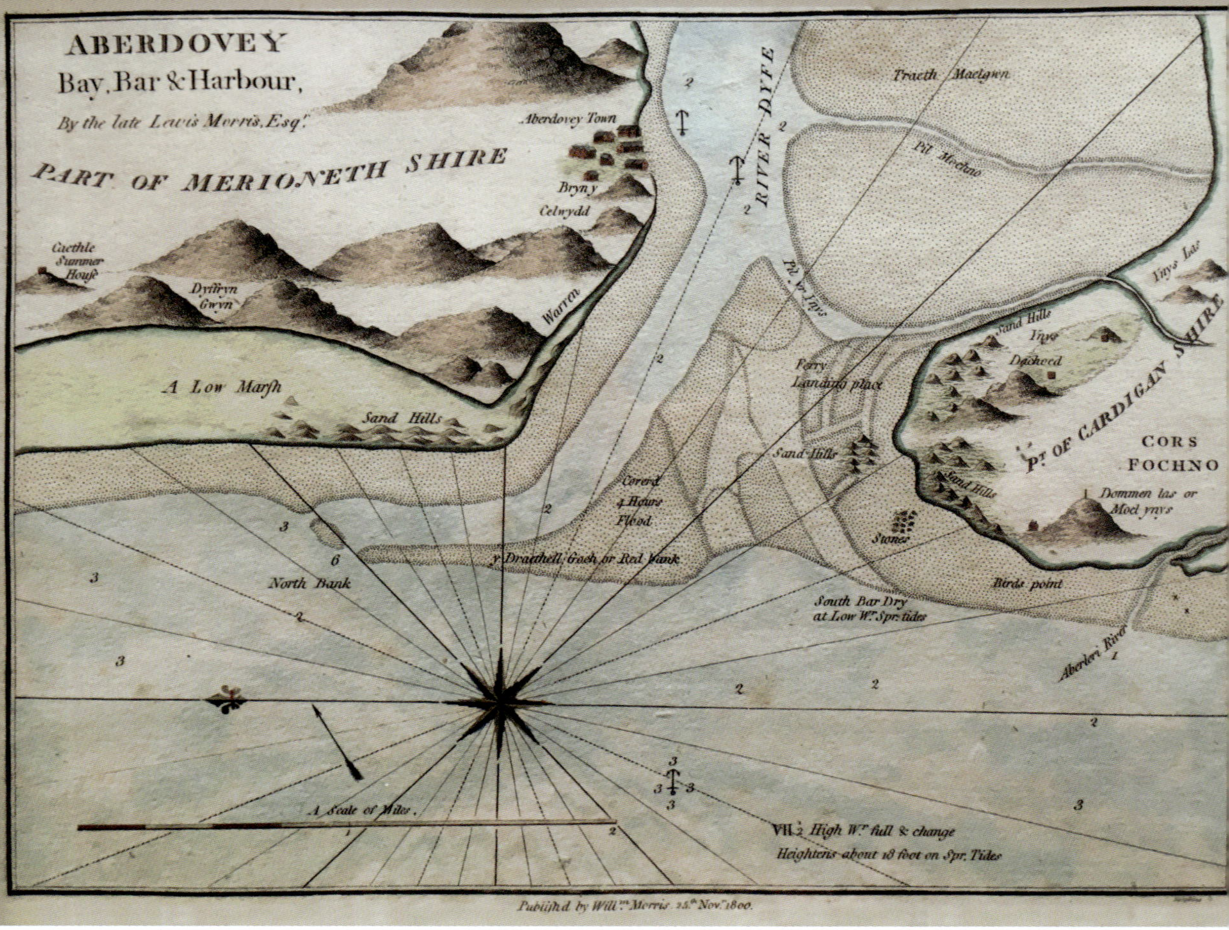

Chart of Aberdovey from Plans of harbours, bars, bays and roads in St. George's Channel, Lewis Morris, 1748 (revised by William Morris, 1801).

The polymath Lewis Morris published the first accurate charts of Welsh harbours and persuaded a reluctant Admiralty to take on continuing responsibility. It shows the narrow harbour entrance as similar to today's, a tiny settlement at Aberdyfi, the ferry, sand dunes and the coastal marsh, as well as an otherwise unmentioned rabbit warren. Lewis Morris (1701–65) was a Welsh hydrographer, antiquary, poet, and prospector of mines who was briefly Collector of Customs for Aberdyfi (1751–56) and presumably lived at the Old Custom House.

centre of Aberdyfi, at Panteidal to the east, and in Cwm Maethlon. Slate quarrying, the final great Dyfi industry, got slowly underway at Aberllefenni, near Corris, in the Dulas valley in the 1780s.

Small river boats and coracles had always been built and used along the river, but coastal trading had relied on ships built and based elsewhere. This changed in the last quarter of the century when local consortia began to commission sea-going boats. Derwenlas had three shipbuilders, and there were also yards at Morben, Llyn Bwtri and on the River Leri. It was a simple process, only needing a space close to the river, a supply of timber, a sawpit, and a stove. The ships were then manned by seafarers from Aberdyfi and Borth who, at first, also had land-based jobs, but were later engaged full time, spending long periods cramped into the tiny vessels.

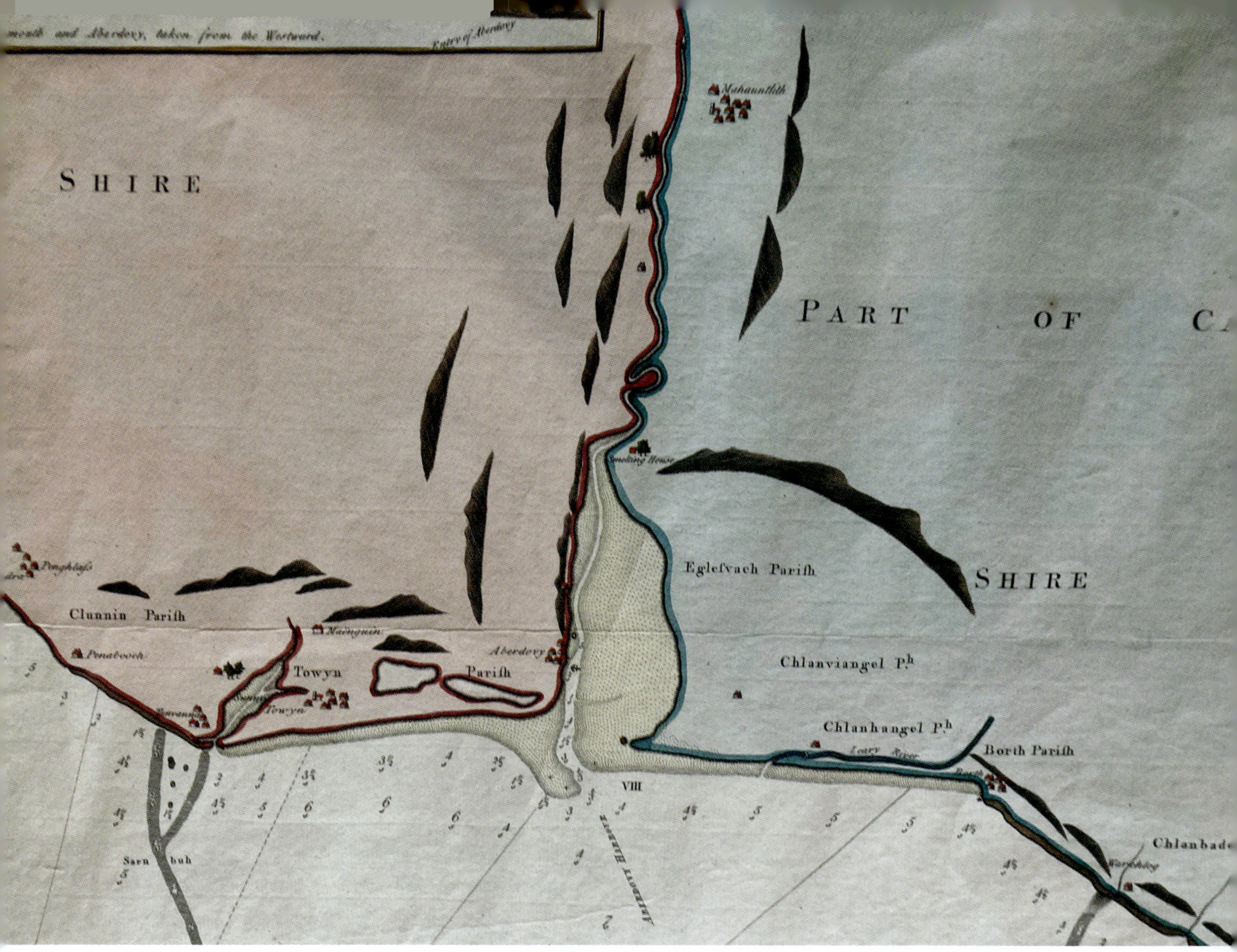

The North Part of Cardigan Bay in Wales, Murdoch Mackenzie, 1775.

This large summary map shows the Dyfi and Dysynni estuaries and areas of marsh outlined in red. Mackenzie contributed more to British hydrography than any other individual, and was appointed Admiralty Surveyor. The more detailed coastal maps based on his surveys, known as the Mackenzie Charts, are in use to this day.

In the mid eighteenth century, the cluster of houses and warehouses at Aberdyfi became a village of miners, mariners and fishermen, which expanded on the only suitable land – up the narrow valley. Anne Owen, the heiress of Ynys y Maengwyn, and her husband developed a triangle of roads with a central space, now Chapel Square, where goods were handled and displayed. Later, there was a stone quayside enabling boats to tie up alongside, and in the early nineteenth century a simple jetty allowing boats to moor in deep water. There was a regional Custom House until it was transferred to Aberystwyth in 1770, and the Ship Inn (now the Dovey Inn), with its date stone of 1729. Terraces of cottages were begun in what became Copper Hill Street, originally thatched and one with a dated plaque (perhaps moved from an older cottage) for 1733. There was still no road, but the first turnpike from Machynlleth to Tywyn was built nearby in 1775 on the line of an old route through Pennal and Cwm Maethlon.

Survey of Ynys y Maengwyn Estate, the property of Henry Arthur Corbet,
Richard Owen, 1776.

This section of one page in an estate atlas shows Aberdyfi village with port buildings on the waterfront, and recent workers' cottages inland along the valley in what became Chapel Square. Soon after this time, the Ynys y Maengwyn estate began to develop copper and lead mines, and the harbour, and later sold parcels of land which enabled the expansion of the village.

Nineteenth-century heyday

Agriculture and fishing continued to be important, but from early in the century Aberdyfi was transformed by industrial, transport and cultural revolutions. It is difficult today to imagine this mid nineteenth-century heyday, with a hubbub of improvement, industry and trade. Along the riverbanks there were smoking chimneys, mills, mines, quarries and new roads. Large areas of marsh were being drained, the waste and commons enclosed. Mining and quarrying reached a peak. Railway navvies built embankments and tunnels along the estuary and through the village.

Industry

There were late eighteenth-century lead mines near Aberdyfi at Caethle (Melin Llyn y Pair) in Cwm Maethlon and Tyddyn Briddell close to Llyn Barfog. Much more ambitiously, from around 1800, Edward Corbet mined copper and lead above Aberdyfi village at Corbet Dovey. Evidence is limited, but some of the workers' cottages may be very late eighteenth-

Corbet to Corbett

Anne and Athelstan Owen's remarkable and colourful grandson, **Edward Corbet** (1741–1820), inherited the Ynys y Maengwyn estate in 1782. Described as a benevolent despot and scourge of the Methodists, he set about improving his land at Tywyn and Aberdyfi by draining marshes, enclosing land, liming, irrigating, crop rotation and breeding cattle and sheep. He began copper and lead mining at Aberdyfi and built the first road along the estuary shore. Among many other interests he was also a great racing man, and Tywyn horse races were famous.

When he died in 1820 he had no legitimate sons, and the estate passed to his nephew, **Athelstan**, who continued building, enclosing and draining land. His main achievements were his promotion of the 1827 turnpike, the Corbet Arms Hotel, and starting to develop Aberdyfi village. On his death in 1835, the estate passed to his sister **Henrietta**, whose daughter married John Soden of Bath, who changed his name to Corbet. In 1871, their son **Athelstan John Soden Corbet** inherited, but poor management of the estate, combined with extravagance, resulted in crippling mortgages and inevitable land sales, including much of Aberdyfi, from 1873.

In 1878, **John Corbett** (1817–1901) of Droitwich, Worcestershire, purchased the estate for £42,000. He was an English industrialist and philanthropist, particularly associated with the salt industry and nicknamed the Salt King. He built the French-style Chateau Impney near Droitwich at a staggering cost. Although he never lived permanently in Tywyn, he was a very large benefactor of the town's physical, social and cultural infrastructure. In Aberdyfi, little of the estate remained, but he paid for a charming porch for the Literary Institute in 1897.

century, and by the time Edward Fenton (see later) visited in 1808, mining was well under way. Corbet also confidently and ambitiously explored for local coal that he could use for smelting his copper, but inevitably failed. The Ynys y Maengwyn estate then leased the mine to a London company from 1823, which smelted elsewhere. Peak production in 1860 was said to be 42 tons, and in 1861 new machinery was installed and allegedly 50 men were working there. However, a sale in 1863 seems to have ended mining. In 1873, the Ynys y Maengwyn estate auctioned Balkan Hill (probably newly named) in several lots. Seven acres, including the mine works, were bought by Captain John Lewis, a retired master mariner, who built Balkan Hill House. The underground mine workings are extensive but there is now no above-ground evidence, other than patches of green copper on several Balkan Hill garden walls.

The Ynys y Maengwyn estate developed an industrial centre of mines and workers' cottages around Copper Hill Street, larger houses for mariners along New Street, and promoted the Pennal to Tywyn turnpike, enabling the building of the church and grander houses on Seaview Terrace.

Ordnance Survey Map, 1 inch, First Edition, 1837.

Aberdyfi lies on a small area of firm flat land at the bottom of a valley, with a smaller valley and harbour at Penhelyg. To the north there is marshland behind the sand dunes. It shows the 1827 turnpike coast road.

Tithe Map 1841, Aberdyfi and Penhelig in Tithe Plan of the parish of Towyn in the County of Merioneth, Thomas Hughes of Llangyniew and Richard Morgan of Talybont, 1841.

Most of the land around Aberdyfi and Penhelyg and further afield was owned by the trustees of the deceased Athelstan Corbet. There is evidence of considerable building along the seafront and around Chapel Square since the construction of the 1827 turnpike and even since the 1837 Ordnance Survey map.

Dyfi industries

Timber products: Timber was important for local use and as a major export. Also oak bark for tanning and as charcoal.

Tanning: Machynlleth, like most market towns, had a considerable leather and tanning industry and there were numerous small tanneries around the estuary, including at Aberdyfi. They benefitted from supplies of heavy leather from cattle, lighter sheep leathers, a water supply from small streams, and oak bark for tanning from local mills.

Wool and cloth: From the mid sixteenth century, Meirionnydd had the raw materials and the water supply to become a centre of cottage-based cloth and flannel making, exporting overland to Shrewsbury. At the end of the eighteenth century, demand increased for cheap Welsh wool and the industry became more organised with mills sited by fast-flowing streams in places like Forge and Talybont. As most of the mill-owners were men of slender resources, their machines were simple and their buildings primitive. Some of their products were exported via Aberdyfi.

Metal mining: In the seventeenth century, north Ceredigion became a major centre of lead and silver mining, with most of the lead exported from Garreg (Glandyfi) on the Dyfi. Copper and lead mining became highly profitable between around 1830 until the 1880s. There were up to a thousand lead mines in Ceredigion and west Montgomeryshire, sending much of their ores by river from Derwenlas and trans-shipping at Aberdyfi – and later by railway. They became less profitable from 1880 as they faced increased international competition, and most closed by 1900. The Aberdyfi copper and lead mines were small and less profitable.

Slate: Quarrying in north Wales began at the end of the eighteenth century with mammoth enterprises at Penrhyn and Bethesda. Slate had also been quarried on a small scale in south Meirionnydd from the earliest times as a local building material. Aberllefenni was the oldest; the two principal nineteenth-century quarries at Corris were Braichgoch and Gaewern, and finally, in the 1860s, Bryneglwys near Abergynolwyn became one of the largest mid Wales quarries, producing at its peak 30 per cent of the south Meirionnydd output.

Success depended upon better transport. First, a network of local tramways, and then, Sir John Edwards of Plas, Machynlleth, built a new road from Machynlleth along the Dulas valley in 1830. Large-scale quarrying took off with the construction, initially, of the horse-drawn tramway connecting Corris quarries with Derwenlas in 1859, the Talyllyn steam railway to Tywyn in 1865, and finally the construction of the Cambrian railway line. However, it was all a bit late, and Corris' quarries never lived up to the more extravagant hopes, or could be compared with great quarries to the north.

Aberdyfi from the north, *c.*1925, with later colouring.

Copper Hill Street has expanded along the valley between Balkan Hill and the ridge that ends in Pen y Bryn lookout. The most recent houses are Tai Newyddion Cottages built for Plas Penhelig staff. The copper mines are beneath the foreground hillside. There is an entrance to the left of the track which is now under a block of flats in Trem y Leri.

A contemporary account

Edward Fenton, who wrote a dairy of travels around Wales, recorded an account of the Aberdyfi mines and of road building in 1808:

Monday, Oct1' 10th. – Left Ynisymangwyn, accompanied by Mr. Corbet and the Ladies to Aberdovey, where I was shewn his Copper Works, now at a stand till his trial for Coal be determined that he may smelt the ore on the Spot. The Works occupy the broken ridge of Hills above the Port and just at the back of the Houses. A great deal of Copper, ready prepared, lies on the Bank. In many places appear old Cavities, supposed to be the Works of the Romans, and in one place, the highest up, where there was an appearance of Ore on the Surface, upon opening they found an old excavation filled up with the Rubbish that had been taken out of it, wherein were found hard Stones worn round by the attrition of used as Mallets to pound the Ore; which seems to imply as if the early Inhabitants, prior to the time of the Romans, had begun their simple operations there, before they had become acquainted with the use of Metal.

The Port belongs to Mr. Corbet. From Aberdovey to Machynlleth a new road is begun, which will skirt the Estuary all the way till it joins the Pennal Road on a dead Level, and will form one of the finest rides in the Kingdom. It will unite with Towyn by way of the sands.

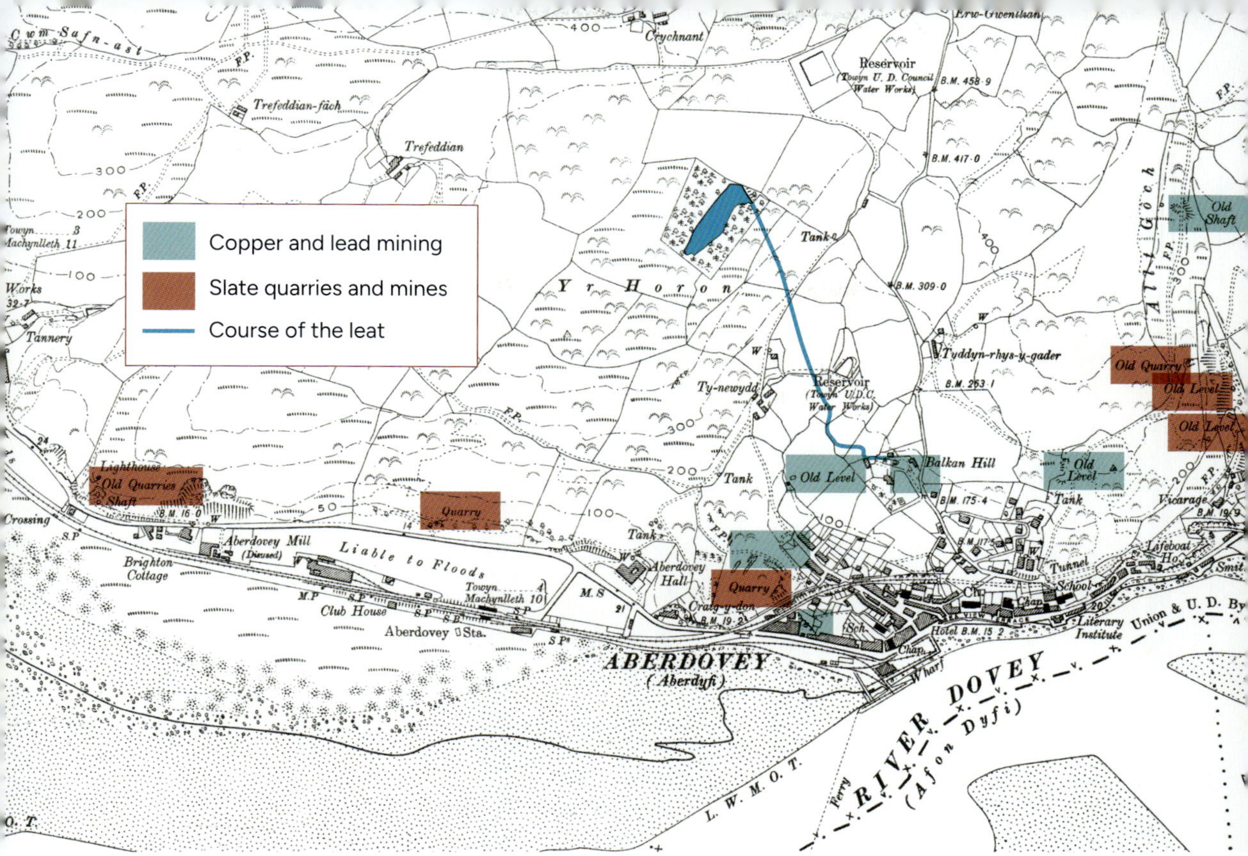

Ordnance Survey Map, 1:2,500, 1902, Merionethshire, Sheet XLVIII.NW

Annotated to show evidence of copper and lead mining together with the course of the leat (stream) from Y Horon reservoir to the mine works and quarrying and slate mines.

Transport

In the early nineteenth century, Aberdyfi's prosperity depended on its continuing river and sea trade. Initially, most imports and exports passed through Derwenlas and were trans-shipped at Aberdyfi. The river was filled with shipping and it was said that when the tide was up, over 80 boats could be seen plying between Derwenlas and Aberdyfi, with their sails up.

After the end of the French wars at Waterloo, trading grew very rapidly, and Samuel Lewis described it in *Topographical Dictionary of Wales*, 1833:

'The River Dovey is navigable to Derwenlas and affords facility of conveying the produce of the quarries and mines to

Abandoned machinery and the green glow of copper inside the Corbet Dovey mine, © Roy Fellows.

Catherine of Aberdovey, E. Jones, oil painting.

A schooner of 76 tons, built in 1869 by John Jones, it was the last ship to be built at Llyn Bwtri. Captain L. Williams, named at the bottom of the picture, lived at Prospect Place, and took command for a short period in 1880.

their destination and of supplying the neighbourhood with various commodities. The average annual exports from this place are 500 tons of bark, 40,000 feet of oak timber, 150,000 yards of oak poles for collieries, 100 tons of lead ore and 1,500 tons of slate. The average annual imports are 5,000 quarters of rye and wheat, 1,000 tons of coal, 500 tons of culm, 2,000 tons of limestone, 11,000 English and foreign hides, and groceries and other shop goods to the amount of £14,000 in value.'

All this needed an enlarged sea-going shipping fleet, and between 1780 and 1840 at least 50 ships were built on the Dyfi, mainly at Derwenlas and nearby. At first, most were sloops with flat bottoms, enabling them to stand upright at low tide in primitive coastal ports, but as deep-sea trade expanded, the size of ships increased and the shipbuilding moved downriver. Aberdyfi eventually had six yards: five from Penhelyg to Trefri, and one on the site of the present Bodfor Terrace. They built some 60 ships, sloops, brigs and schooners between 1840 and 1880.

Aberdyfi and Borth developed a vibrant maritime community of sailors, shipwrights, carpenters, boatmen, ferrymen and customs officers. Their seafarers sailed the high seas

Ink sketch of Aberdyfi from Ynys Las, F. Wood, *c.*1840.

From the left: The Corbet Arms, Craig y don, the first Glandyfi Terrace houses and the harbour and village. The western approach to the village was dominated by marshes and frequently flooded, and there was little building until after the railway embankment.

around the British Isles to Europe, and across the Atlantic. Lewis Lloyd, the historian of Dyfi shipping, recorded 543 mariners, 46 shipbuilders and 37 boatmen (sea fishermen, ferrymen and pilots) during the busiest period of 1750 to 1850, mostly living in Aberdyfi or Borth.

Roads

Until the nineteenth century, most of the north shore was only accessible by boat or farm tracks over the hills. Then came new roads. In 1808, Edward Corbet built Hen Ffordd Corbet, just above the tidal level, from Pennal to Aberdyfi, to carry ore from his planned new mines. Blasted through rock at a low level by demobilised troops from Wellington's army, it very quickly failed as the tides washed away the road surface. A few short stretches survive the building of the railway and English tourists were told that it was a Roman road.

Edward Corbet's nephew, Athelstan Corbet, who inherited the estate in 1820, then promoted a more ambitious new turnpike at a higher level, putting in £2,000 of his own money and obtaining a government grant of £1,000. It was planned by Thomas Penson (1790–1859), a prolific and versatile Oswestry architect and surveyor of roads, and was completed in 1827 after two years of major engineering. Samuel Lewis described this spectacular corniche road in the 1849 edition of his *Topographical Dictionary of Wales*: 'For nearly the whole of its extent from Pennal to Aberdyfi, it is cut through solid rock, which in many places presents its naked side, of different elevations, forming a pleasing contrast to the wooded declivity of the hill, presenting, in conjunction with the broad estuary of the river, a scene of picturesque beauty.' It remains the basis of the present narrow and winding main road.

Looking up Afon Dyfi along the turnpike from Penhelyg, John Thomas, *c.*1890.

The turnpike to Pennal with Plas Trefri and Braich y Celyn in the distance, and remains of the Corbet road by the waterside.

The Corbet road, *c.*1808, at Abertafol.

Stretches of road can still be seen at Penhelyg and around headlands along the estuary shore, but most have been lost to the railway.

New roads made travel easier. A twice-weekly coach service began in 1827 between Welshpool, Newtown, Machynlleth, Aberdyfi and Tywyn, and encouraged travellers to visit and enjoy the scenery and natural history. They also enabled the next stage of expansion of the village along the newly-created waterfront: the church in 1837, chapels, the grander houses of Seaview Terrace, a lifeboat house, and two taverns, the Britannia Inn and the Penhelig Arms.

The railway

The next and greatest upheaval was the railway. In the 1860s mid Wales joined the standard-gauge railway network formed in the English railway boom of the 1840s. The first section completed, in 1862, was a line from Newtown to Machynlleth. The proposed next stage was to be for a railway along the southern shore of the estuary towards Aberystwyth, with a viaduct from Ynyslas to Aberdyfi and a northern coastal line to beyond Pwllheli. It turned out to be a complicated and fraught story.

Construction brought in hundreds of navvies and caused massive disruption. Riverboats contributed to their own demise, taking the materials and supplies from Aberdyfi to Derwenlas and Ynyslas. Financial and engineering problems meant the viaduct plan was abandoned in 1863, and replaced by the Aberdyfi deviation which began with a bridge and station at Dovey Junction and then ran along the north bank of the river. There were then

Penhelyg harbour looking to the centre of the village, *c.*1880.

The harbour is reduced in size since the construction of the railway. Beyond, the 1827 turnpike has been cut into the cliff side which later allowed houses to be built along the roadside. The Penhelig Arms is on the right.

Workers on the wharf, John Thomas, *c.*1885.

angry disputes between residents, the Ynys y Maengwyn estate, and the railway company over proposals to route the line along the Aberdyfi waterfront. Eventually, an alternative path around the back of the village was agreed, even though it required steep gradients, sharp curves, three tunnels and bypassed the new Aberdyfi harbour station.

The construction of the railway, with tunnels, a cutting and embankments, caused havoc, but it really did change everything. It put an end to river transport, but created a small industrial port, even though it was another 20 years before there was a new wharf and jetty. Aberdyfi continued to be the main route for the export of slate and the import of coal, limestone and timber until the First World War. It also meant that Aberdyfi would, like Aberystwyth and Barmouth, develop as a resort for the middle classes of the English Midlands.

Social change: Nonconformism and tourism

At least as important as the industrial and transport revolution and new building were profound political and social changes: the decline of the gentry estates, local government, Nonconformism, tourism, education and a revival of the Welsh language. People became more involved with a wider world.

Nonconformism brought with it a ruthless stamping out of the old robust ways of life, and changed beliefs, behaviour and politics. Instead, it promoted temperance, education,

View across the estuary, engraving, Newman & Co., 1860.

The construction of the railway at Aberdyfi

- **1862:** Machynlleth to Ynyslas and then beyond to Aberystwyth.
- **1862:** A ferry branch line from Ynyslas to the estuary edge as a temporary route for the Dyfi ferry and to bring in building materials.
- **1863:** A section of the northern line between Aberdyfi harbour and Llwyngwril to the north of Tywyn.
- **1863:** The Dyfi viaduct plan abandoned and replaced by construction of the deviation line. The steamer *SS Elizabeth* purchased to carry railway passengers across the river between Ynyslas and Aberdyfi.
- **1865–6:** The owners of Bryneglwys Quarry, near Abergynolwyn, build a narrow-gauge railway to Tywyn where a connection with the new standard gauge Aberdyfi line enables slate to be carried to ships. It was the world's first narrow-gauge railway designed for locomotives.
- **1866:** The mainline deviation completed and connected to the harbour branch which runs back to the wharf and jetty in the village. A horsebus and, later, a small motorbus take passengers into the village.
- **1867:** The northern line to Pwllheli completed.

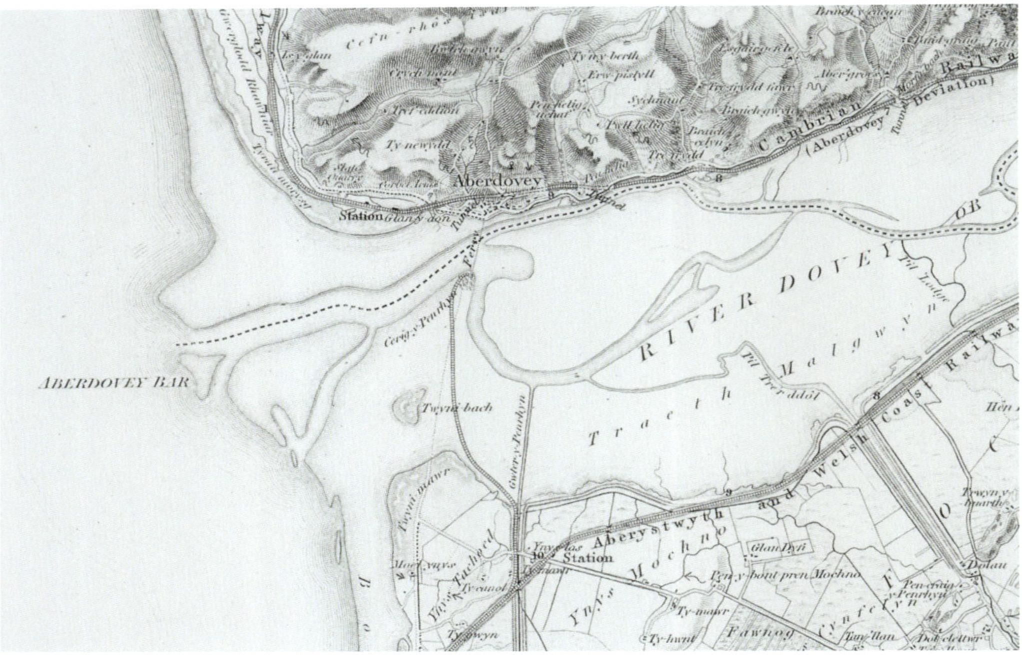

Ordnance Survey, 1st Edition Revised, 1890. With recently completed railway tracks including the temporary Ynyslas ferry branch.

choral singing and Sabbatarianism, all of which would come to be seen as characteristically Welsh. The Anglican Church also began to revive and Aberdyfi became a new parish with a handsome church.

Tourism

The roads and railway opened the prospect for an entirely new source of income – tourism. In 1829, Athelstan Corbet optimistically built the Corbet Arms Family Hotel and Post House on the edge of the sea at the western end of Aberdyfi. However, most visitors stayed in lodging houses temporarily vacated by their owners. After a slow start, by 1854, Evan Jones of Machynlleth could describe much greater activity: 'Aberdyfi is frequented by large hordes of respectable visitors. Comfortable lodgings for families can be found here; the Corbet Arms Hotel is a spacious and convenient place which is kept clean and tidy. It has recently attracted significant attention as a suitable winter residence for the clergy. The breeze is mild and pleasing, and the weather usually agreeable and wholesome. The beach is magnificent, and composed of hard sand, such that a carriage can travel safely on it for about six miles.'

There were new attractions, such as bathing huts. From 1840 there was horse racing on the sands and an Aberdyfi regatta under the patronage of Mr Wynne of Peniarth and the Marquess of Londonderry of Plas, Machynlleth, who in 1872 graced the occasion in his luxurious 506-ton steam yacht, *Maglona*.

An increasing number of visitors meant that difficult to pronounce Welsh place-names began to be replaced by banal English names in guidebooks and by lodging houses, carriage proprietors and others. We still have the Happy Valley, the Roman Road, Picnic Island, and many others. Intended only for visitors, there were concerns that the historic Welsh names were being lost as English became the language of local government, education and of English incomers. Many thought that the Welsh language would, and even should, not survive. Yet it has and Welsh is the first language of many Aberdyfi residents.

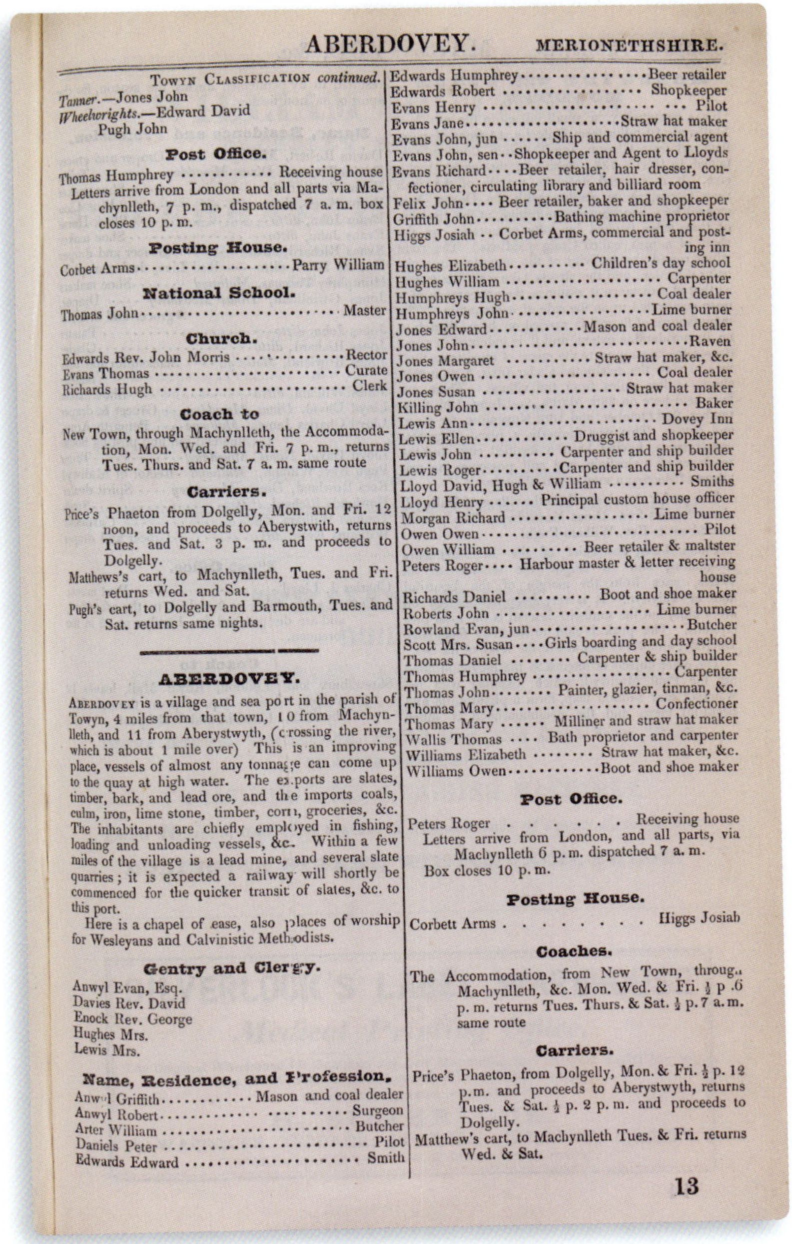

ABERDOVEY. MERIONETHSHIRE.

TOWYN CLASSIFICATION *continued.*

Tanner.—Jones John
Wheelwrights.—Edward David
Pugh John

Post Office.

Thomas Humphrey ············ Receiving house
Letters arrive from London and all parts via Machynlleth, 7 p. m., dispatched 7 a. m. box closes 10 p. m.

Posting House.

Corbet Arms ···················· Parry William

National School.

Thomas John ························ Master

Church.

Edwards Rev. John Morris ················ Rector
Evans Thomas ························ Curate
Richards Hugh ························ Clerk

Coach to

New Town, through Machynlleth, the Accommodation, Mon. Wed. and Fri. 7 p. m., returns Tues. Thurs. and Sat. 7 a. m. same route

Carriers.

Price's Phaeton from Dolgelly, Mon. and Fri. 12 noon, and proceeds to Aberystwith, returns Tues. and Sat. 3 p. m. and proceeds to Dolgelly.
Matthews's cart, to Machynlleth, Tues. and Fri. returns Wed. and Sat.
Pugh's cart, to Dolgelly and Barmouth, Tues. and Sat. returns same nights.

ABERDOVEY.

ABERDOVEY is a village and sea port in the parish of Towyn, 4 miles from that town, 10 from Machynlleth, and 11 from Aberystwyth, (crossing the river, which is about 1 mile over) This is an improving place, vessels of almost any tonnage can come up to the quay at high water. The exports are slates, timber, bark, and lead ore, and the imports coals, culm, iron, lime stone, timber, corn, groceries, &c. The inhabitants are chiefly employed in fishing, loading and unloading vessels, &c. Within a few miles of the village is a lead mine, and several slate quarries; it is expected a railway will shortly be commenced for the quicker transit of slates, &c. to this port.

Here is a chapel of ease, also places of worship for Wesleyans and Calvinistic Methodists.

Gentry and Clergy.

Anwyl Evan, Esq.
Davies Rev. David
Enock Rev. George
Hughes Mrs.
Lewis Mrs.

Name, Residence, and Profession.

Anwyl Griffith ············ Mason and coal dealer
Anwyl Robert ······················ Surgeon
Arter William ······················ Butcher
Daniels Peter ························ Pilot
Edwards Edward ······················ Smith
Edwards Humphrey ················ Beer retailer
Edwards Robert ················· Shopkeeper
Evans Henry ························ Pilot
Evans Jane ··················· Straw hat maker
Evans John, jun ······ Ship and commercial agent
Evans John, sen ·· Shopkeeper and Agent to Lloyds
Evans Richard ···· Beer retailer, hair dresser, confectioner, circulating library and billiard room
Felix John ···· Beer retailer, baker and shopkeeper
Griffith John ·········· Bathing machine proprietor
Higgs Josiah ·· Corbet Arms, commercial and posting inn
Hughes Elizabeth ·········· Children's day school
Hughes William ····················· Carpenter
Humphreys Hugh ··················· Coal dealer
Humphreys John ··················· Lime burner
Jones Edward ············ Mason and coal dealer
Jones John ·························· Raven
Jones Margaret ··········· Straw hat maker, &c.
Jones Owen ························ Coal dealer
Jones Susan ················· Straw hat maker
Killing John ·························· Baker
Lewis Ann ························ Dovey Inn
Lewis Ellen ············ Druggist and shopkeeper
Lewis John ·········· Carpenter and ship builder
Lewis Roger ·········· Carpenter and ship builder
Lloyd David, Hugh & William ·········· Smiths
Lloyd Henry ······ Principal custom house officer
Morgan Richard ··················· Lime burner
Owen Owen ···························· Pilot
Owen William ·········· Beer retailer & maltster
Peters Roger ···· Harbour master & letter receiving house
Richards Daniel ·········· Boot and shoe maker
Roberts John ······················ Lime burner
Rowland Evan, jun ···················· Butcher
Scott Mrs. Susan ···· Girls boarding and day school
Thomas Daniel ········ Carpenter & ship builder
Thomas Humphrey ···················· Carpenter
Thomas John ········ Painter, glazier, tinman, &c.
Thomas Mary ······················ Confectioner
Thomas Mary ······ Milliner and straw hat maker
Wallis Thomas ···· Bath proprietor and carpenter
Williams Elizabeth ········ Straw hat maker, &c.
Williams Owen ············ Boot and shoe maker

Post Office.

Peters Roger . . . . Receiving house
Letters arrive from London, and all parts, via Machynlleth 6 p. m. dispatched 7 a. m.
Box closes 10 p. m.

Posting House.

Corbett Arms . . . . Higgs Josiah

Coaches.

The Accommodation, from New Town, through Machynlleth, &c. Mon. Wed. & Fri. ½ p. 6 p. m. returns Tues. Thurs. & Sat. ½ p. 7 a. m. same route

Carriers.

Price's Phaeton, from Dolgelly, Mon. & Fri. ½ p. 12 p.m. and proceeds to Aberystwyth, returns Tues. & Sat. ½ p. 2 p. m. and proceeds to Dolgelly.
Matthew's cart, to Machynlleth Tues. & Fri. returns Wed. & Sat.

13

'Aberdovey', in *Robinson's Trade Directory*, 1840.

The list of residents and their businesses in *Robinson's Trade Directory* provides a picture of a busy working port, but with a few hints of a different future: the Corbet Arms, proprietors of bathing machines and of a bathhouse, and Mrs Scott's Boarding School for Young Ladies.

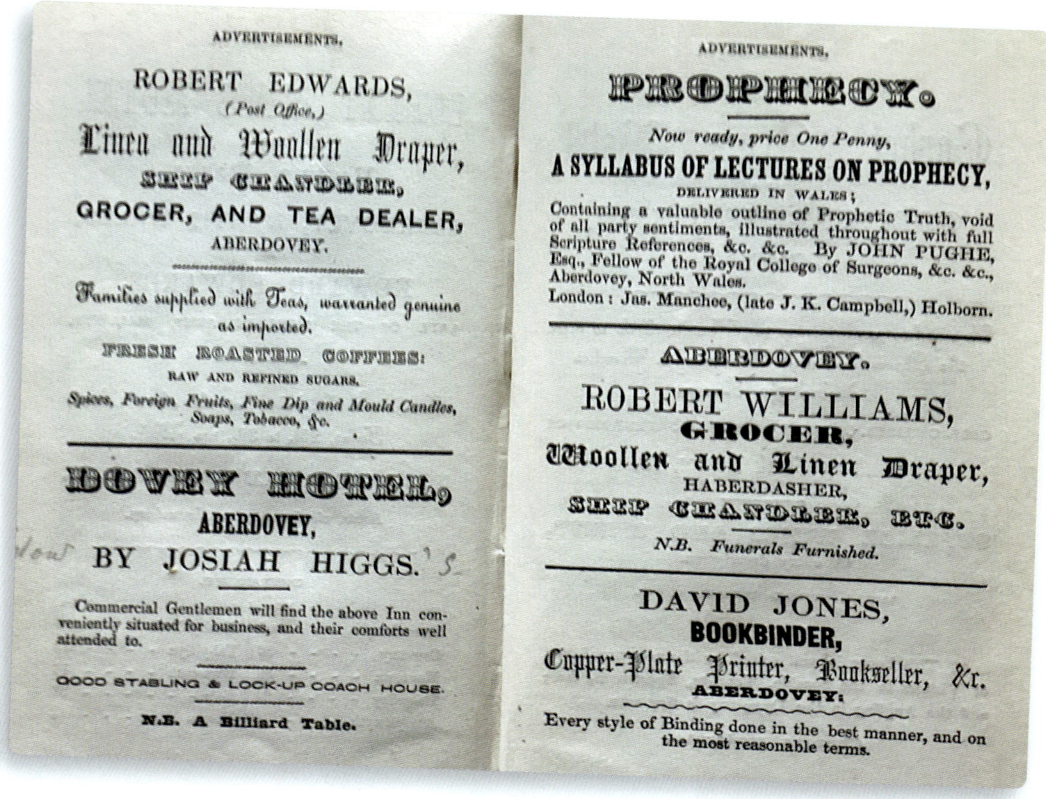

ADVERTISEMENTS.

ROBERT EDWARDS,
(Post Office,)
Linen and Woollen Draper,
SHIP CHANDLER,
GROCER, AND TEA DEALER,
ABERDOVEY.

Families supplied with Teas, warranted genuine as imported.
FRESH ROASTED COFFEES:
RAW AND REFINED SUGARS,
Spices, Foreign Fruits, Fine Dip and Mould Candles, Soaps, Tobacco, &c.

DOVEY HOTEL,
ABERDOVEY,
BY JOSIAH HIGGS.

Commercial Gentlemen will find the above Inn conveniently situated for business, and their comforts well attended to.

GOOD STABLING & LOCK-UP COACH HOUSE.

N.B. A Billiard Table.

ADVERTISEMENTS.

PROPHECY.

Now ready, price One Penny,
A SYLLABUS OF LECTURES ON PROPHECY,
DELIVERED IN WALES;
Containing a valuable outline of Prophetic Truth, void of all party sentiments, illustrated throughout with full Scripture References, &c. &c. By JOHN PUGHE, Esq., Fellow of the Royal College of Surgeons, &c. &c., Aberdovey, North Wales.
London: Jas. Manchee, (late J. K. Campbell,) Holborn.

ABERDOVEY.
ROBERT WILLIAMS,
GROCER,
Woollen and Linen Draper,
HABERDASHER,
SHIP CHANDLER, ETC.
N.B. Funerals Furnished.

DAVID JONES,
BOOKBINDER,
Copper-Plate Printer, Bookseller, &c.
ABERDOVEY:
Every style of Binding done in the best manner, and on the most reasonable terms.

Page of advertisements in *Guide to Aberdovey*, Thomas Owen Morgan, 1854.

The collapse of industry

In the second half of the nineteenth century, the established bases of the local economy – agriculture and industry – declined. Even so, Aberdyfi port continued to export slate and import coal, limestone and timber until the First World War. The first steamer visited in 1834 and steam replaced sail by the 1870s. For a while, the Aberdovey and Barmouth Steamship Company, founded in 1877, provided a regular and well-loved passenger and goods service to Liverpool and Ireland, with *SS Telephone* and *SS Dora* – until finally *Dora* was requisitioned in 1916. However, hopes of becoming a major port between Ireland and the Midlands were doomed to failure.

Fishing for the autumn herring and other sea fishing continued, and mussels and shellfish were harvested. Salmon and sewin (sea trout) were abundant, and upriver there was outrage from around 1840 at the attempts of the Wynnstay estate to control and limit fishing by local people. Fishing in the tidal estuary was different, and salmon and sewin were netted in deeper pools from small boats and coracles. In 1880, there were a dozen teams based at Glandyfi and at Aberdyfi, fishing the estuary.

As industry and river trade declined, tourism prospered, and wealthy incomers built houses on the edge of the village. The building of lodging houses also accelerated along

1851: A year of change and of a census

D.W. Morgan, Aberdyfi's historian, wrote: 'The memorable year that witnessed the great Slate and Shipping Boom was the year 1851 ... unexampled prosperity came to the quarries and the shipyards, continuing unabated for 26 years.' It was also 'the period when tourism and new housing for incomers began to take off.'

The ten-yearly census for 1851 is a picture of a seafaring village of 155 households, immediately before change. The population (excluding the outlying farms) was 580, of whom 203 were of school age or less, and 31 were paupers. Most of the men were or had been mariners (16), boatmen (4), pilots (5), or ferrymen (3). Ten were employed in shipbuilding. Mining seems to have largely finished, with only five men working in Aberdyfi or other mines. There is no indication of the imminent slate trade.

There were innkeepers at the Dovey Hotel, the Britannia, and the Penhelig Arms; and a range of shopkeepers and tradesmen similar to the 1840 Robinson's list. There is little evidence of provision for an increasing number of visitors, apart from the Corbet Arms and two lodging houses, but other houses would have been reorganised to become boarding houses in the summer.

There were very few households that might have been generously classified as gentry: the surgeon, Dr John Pughe, at Penhelig House (now Lodge); Mrs Ann Pughe, proprietor of a lead mine (Dylife) at Brynawel; the Rev. Morgan, vicar of St Peter's Church at Craig y Don, and one 'landed proprietor'. Twenty-four of the 155 households had live-in servants, usually only one, though the widowed Mrs Ann Pughe had two servants and a coachman, and the vicar had a cook, housemaid and nursemaid.

the seafront: to the east to Penhelyg and beyond, and then to the west with late nineteenth-century Glandyfi and Bodfor Terraces. The railway brought both excursion trains and visitors to stay.

A still-busy port, a growing village, and successful tourism meant many changes. Chapels were rebuilt. There were new shops, some of whose original fronts survive: the wonderful Medical Hall (1863), Aberdyfi Butchers, and Liverpool House. The Calvinistic Methodist chapel in Chapel Square was converted in 1864 to an Assembly Room. The early nineteenth-century bath house and Plymouth Brethren chapel became the Literary Institute in 1882.

The historic power of the gentry and clergy was replaced with new local government. Education was made compulsory and there were two new primary schools. There were the beginnings of public services: gas works (with a lamplighter) in 1868, and a reservoir above the village to supply water in 1898 and, much later, electricity from Cwm Maethlon in 1945.

During all this activity the Ynys y Maengwyn estate, now held in trust, 'was increasingly troubled' from the mid 1850s. In the late 1870s the trustees sold land on the Aberdyfi hillsides in a numerous lots before selling the rest of their estate to John Corbett of

A view of Aberdovey from Pen y Bryn (Head of the Hill), lithograph, after A.F. Goddard, *c.*1860.

The centre of the village before the railway. There is a stagecoach on Seaview Terrace.

Droitwich in 1878. Thereafter, the more enterprising new owners were responsible for lodging houses on Glandyfi and Bodfor Terraces, and then for rather different developments – a new demand for detached villas with gardens as retirement and second homes. At first, along Balkan Hill in the 1890s; at the very end of the century a whole group of houses with large gardens in a new Hopeland Road.

There were new activities for visitors. Picturesque walks with picturesque names. A local landowner gave the shelter that still dominates Pen y Bryn. And then there was what became the outstanding golf links.

One of the oldest courses in Wales, it dates from the early 1880s. Colonel Arthur Ruck, who was spending his annual leave with his parents who were in the habit of spending the winter at Aberdyfi, found a good piece of common land and, using nine flowerpots for holes, made a course where he introduced golf to a handful of locals, relatives and friends. Arthur Ruck's brother, Richard Matthews Ruck, a Royal Engineer, soon took over, using his skills to lay out the 18-hole course on marshy common ground. He then organised the foundation of the club in 1892. The club was able to acquire ownership of the former common land for £2,250 in 1905 after disputes with property developing claimants of the manorial rights. The club then completed drainage of the marsh.

Salmon fishermen at Aberdyfi, John Thomas, *c.*1885.

The netting of salmon became more important as unemployed mariners turned to estuary fishing and the gathering of mussels.

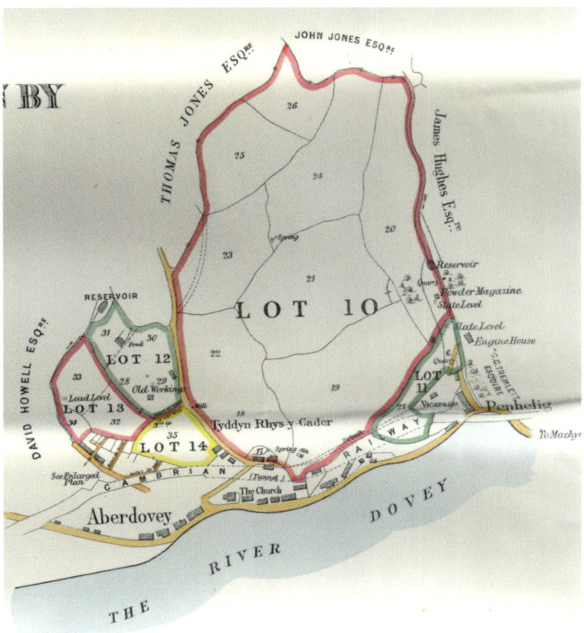

Map from the particulars for a sale by William Dew Auctioneers, at the Corbet Arms, Tywyn, 8 August 1879, on behalf of the Trustees and Executors of the late A.J.S. Corbet Esq, of outlying areas of the Ynys y Maengwyn estate.

There were 14 lots in Aberdyfi. Lot 12 was the site of the mine works. Lot 9 was a timber yard on Terrace Road. The brief descriptions include several comments on development potential.

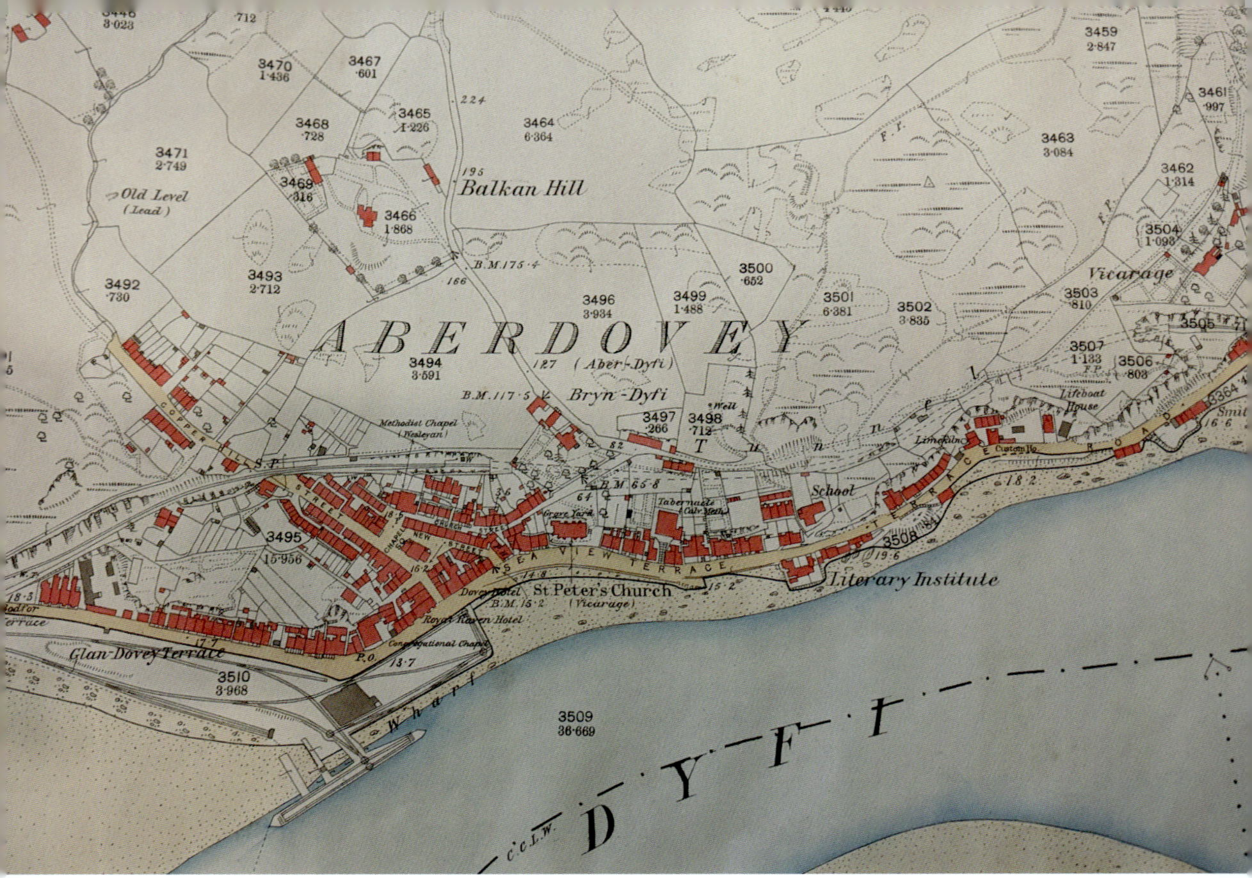

Ordnance Survey Map, 25 inch, First Edition, 1889.

The village has grown along the waterfront and there are the beginnings of new housing on the hillside.

Early twentieth century

The first 40 years of the twentieth century saw the final demise of coastal shipping and of the traditional occupations depending on the sea; and a general decline in fishing. Aberdyfi now increasingly depended on being a home for wealthy new residents and second home owners, and a resort for visitors from the English Midlands. There were new activities and the harbour filled with privately owned boats. Signor Marconi was a frequent visitor to the port in his splendid yacht *Elettra* when working at his Long Wave wireless receiver station in Tywyn.

The building boom was both infill and new roads around the edge of the older village: Hopeland Avenue, Penhelig Terrace, Gwelfor Road and Philip Avenue. Plas Penhelig was the grandest house of all, gabled with a veranda, glasshouses and outhouses, surrounded by very large gardens and with extensive accommodation for a large staff. The success of the golf course was followed by the Trefeddian Hotel (named after a nearby farm) in 1904.

When Britain declared war on Germany on 4 August 1914, there was unprecedented government intervention in everyday life. Young men volunteered or were conscripted for

Some of the original members of Aberdovey Golf Club, 1892.

On a sunny day of hard frost, they skated in the morning on nearby marshland and played golf in the afternoon. There was a photographer present, so the party threw down their skates, the president teed off in the largest bunker (facing the wrong way) and the others posed. Among those in the photograph are W.V. Thomas, the owner of Medical Hall, the president, Richard Ruck, and his young brother-in-law, Frank Darwin (son of the naturalist Charles Darwin), and Darwin's son Bernard.

military service. Their absence, together with rationing and restrictions, and the need to increase food production, made great demands. Farming was regulated, with wage and price control, and incentives for mechanisation and good husbandry (such as hedging and ditching). The shortage of labour meant a much greater role for women, and eventually the arrival of the first Land Girls in 1918. The war memorials record the loss of life. Many others were wounded, and the influenza pandemic of 1918 caused more deaths and disability. Few families were untouched.

After the war, Aberdyfi was again a peaceful place. Hugh Lewis, the prolific historian of the village, remembers and describes a simple, neighbourly and self-sufficient childhood. But the village was also growing and changing. More detached homes appeared on the hillsides behind and on the approaches to the village. There was a fine football pitch, and Aberdovey Bowling Club was founded in 1921 with lawn bowls, tennis courts, putting green and a croquet lawn. With the collapse of shipping, men took to sea and river fishing, together with raking the riverbed for mussels in winter.

Cultural changes, which had begun before the war, were obvious: changes in the social structure and in the role of women, and increasing awareness and involvement in the world. There were regular bus services. The cinema at Tywyn, in the former Assembly Rooms, was one of the first in Britain, and there was another at Machynlleth. There were village choirs and meetings and performances at the Imperial Hall and the Literary Institute. People bought gramophones and radios, and a few had telephones. By 1920, motor cars were seen most days, and Gray Jones Garage opened on Terrace Road.

Nonconformism fought against the expectations of an influx of pleasure-seeking tourists, golfers and owners of second homes, and the village remained firmly in favour of temperance and of Sunday closing of shops, entertainment, pubs and golf. One flashpoint was the battle of Aberdovey Golf Club. The club's finances were in a parlous state and they resolved to begin Sunday golf to attract weekend players from the Midlands. There was an outcry. When Sunday play began in October 1927, large crowds obstructed golfers, and a farmer tethered a mountain ram on the 17th green. On Christmas Eve the course was vandalised, with Merry Xmas carved on a green. Legal proceedings began but eventually calm was restored and Sunday play continued. It was noted in the club records that many of the younger protesters were happy to earn extra money by caddying on Sunday mornings.

The Second World War to the present day

War had dramatic consequences for the village. Windows were blacked out and street signs were removed. Petrol and food were rationed. Cardigan Bay unexpectedly found itself in the frontline, facing possible invasion via neutral Ireland. In Nazi Germany the Wehrmacht compiled photographs and maps. There was a major programme of building beach defences, and numerous remnants can still be seen. There was rapid build-up of the military, and Tywyn became, almost overnight, a garrison town with requisitioned houses and public buildings. Convoys of tanks and amphibious vehicles passed up and down the narrow winding roads.

Agriculture was planned. There was mechanisation, further drainage of Cors Fochno, and large areas were ploughed. Women worked on the land and in factories and were eventually joined by Land Girls and by Lumber Jills. On the home front, hundreds of evacuees arrived at Machynlleth by train. People volunteered as Air Raid Wardens (ARP), with the Women's Voluntary Services (WVS), and joined the Home Guard. Schools occupied Trefeddian Hotel and large houses. In a farming area with a river filled with abundant fish, black market food was readily available. However, people also became more self-sufficient: growing vegetables, gathering wild mushrooms and blackberries, keeping pigs and catching rabbits.

As the threat of invasion receded at the end of 1942, the military emphasis changed to training the forces needed to recover occupied Europe. The coast was used by artillery, and the estuary was an ideal terrain for testing equipment and training troops for amphibious landings. The RAF trained in the sky. There were several plane crashes in the hills behind Aberdyfi and Pennal, and the RAF put up a beacon which flashed day and night.

Mr Davies at war

'Mr Davies would like you to go to Aberdyfi to take the post of second engineer on the *Camroux III*,' said George Wood, my chief engineer... Aberdyfi at this time was a very busy place. The jetty was three times the size that it is today. We were alongside the jetty and so was the training ship belonging to the Outward Bound Sea School. At anchor in the river were *Golden Valley* and a Dutch ship. There were thousands of troops training for the coming invasion of Europe. There were many six-wheeled amphibian vehicles called DUKS... All windows in Aberdyfi were criss-crossed with sticky tape, but many had been broken by explosions on Ynyslas beach when they tested things... One fine Sunday afternoon, shortly after my arrival, I decided to take a walk up the hill and came to a little farm. I found out later that it was called Bwlch... Soon a very pretty young lady approached. 'Hello,' she said. 'Hello,' I replied, 'and may I have a cup of tea, please?' 'Yes,' she said, 'and would you like some bacon and eggs, fried bread, followed by some leycakes and jam?' ... We all loved the place, and not only the place, five of us married local girls.

From a memoir by **William Selby Davies**.

By permission from his daughter, Megan Reynolds.

There was also fun. The presence of so many young men made it a lively time. Lorries would collect local girls to take them to dances, and servicemen and women would go out to farmhouses (where rationing seemed unknown) for bacon and eggs.

At the end of the war, Ynyslas had a highly secret role in rocket research and development, which still continues elsewhere. It involved extensive installations at Ynyslas and on *HMS Camroux III*, a requisitioned coaster, anchored at Aberdyfi. There was much firing of rockets onto the mudflats and recording of their landing sites.

In the years following the Second World War, you approached Aberdyfi down quiet, narrow roads between grass verges. It was a smaller, more peaceful place of grey houses with a dilapidated wharf. There were railway sidings and coal wagons in front of Bodfor Terrace, and the newly-founded Dovey Yacht Club in an old air raid shelter. There were several grocers, including one in the corner house at Penhelyg, two banks, and Gray Jones petrol station and garage on Terrace Road. Aberdyfi was then Aberdovey and all the road signs were in English. There was strict Sunday observance with closed shops and pubs. Squads of Outward Bound boys were marched, usually at the double, to the wharf in all weathers. There were familiar people from the longstanding Aberdyfi families. Ellis Williams was ferryman and harbourmaster.

Aberdyfi is now much changed, of course – overwhelmed in summer and empty and intimate in winter. The rebuilt wharf of 1968–71 has new warehouses, the yacht club, lifeboat house and the information centre. There are fewer fishing boats or larger yachts. The village police station has become Copper Cottage. The Outward Bound centre has evolved, making major contributions to mountain rescue and the lifeboat. There are caravan sites, many new houses of uncertain distinction, more cafés and many alterations to the formerly uniform terraces. And it is much more colourful. And the first view of the village and harbour, as one drives along the estuary corniche and then rounds the corner, is still incomparable.

The years since the Second World War have seen a decline in the permanent population, fewer houses only used as second homes, the loss of traditional shops and the closure of the school. But there has been a great increase in the number of houses owned and adapted for short holiday lets. New building has spread up the hillside and to the west, with mobile homes in the sand dunes. The 2021 census found a population of 532 in the village (682 in the parish) of which 43 per cent were Welsh speaking. Forty-three per cent of houses were holiday or letting homes, the highest proportion in Gwynedd.

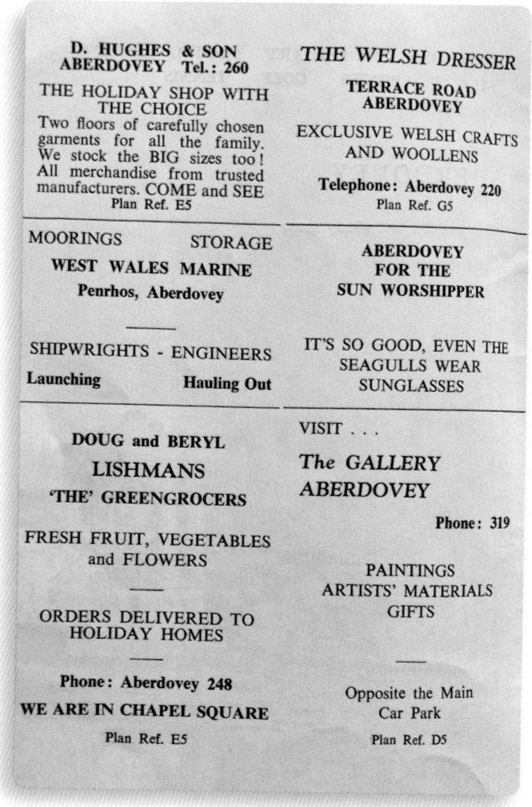

D. HUGHES & SON
ABERDOVEY Tel.: 260
THE HOLIDAY SHOP WITH THE CHOICE
Two floors of carefully chosen garments for all the family. We stock the BIG sizes too! All merchandise from trusted manufacturers. COME and SEE
Plan Ref. E5

THE WELSH DRESSER
TERRACE ROAD
ABERDOVEY
EXCLUSIVE WELSH CRAFTS AND WOOLLENS
Telephone: Aberdovey 220
Plan Ref. G5

MOORINGS STORAGE
WEST WALES MARINE
Penrhos, Aberdovey
SHIPWRIGHTS - ENGINEERS
Launching Hauling Out

ABERDOVEY
FOR THE
SUN WORSHIPPER
IT'S SO GOOD, EVEN THE SEAGULLS WEAR SUNGLASSES

DOUG and BERYL
LISHMANS
'THE' GREENGROCERS
FRESH FRUIT, VEGETABLES and FLOWERS
ORDERS DELIVERED TO HOLIDAY HOMES
Phone: Aberdovey 248
WE ARE IN CHAPEL SQUARE
Plan Ref. E5

VISIT . . .
The GALLERY
ABERDOVEY
Phone: 319
PAINTINGS
ARTISTS' MATERIALS
GIFTS
Opposite the Main Car Park
Plan Ref. D5

Advertisements from a post-war village guide.

(opposite) **Aberdyfi from Ynyslas – A view from a microlight**, © Glyn Davies.

The River Leri, moved and canalised in 1824, enters the estuary bottom right. Coastal sand dunes are continuing to develop on Ynyslas.

Chapter Three

Walking Aberdyfi

The dramatic corniche drive along the Dyfi estuary culminates in a sudden right turn which reveals the surprise of a highly picturesque village clinging to the hillside ahead and below. At first it appears to be entirely nineteenth and twentieth century, but this book has shown that it conceals layers of history: millennia of trade and later a fishing harbour, an entrepôt for Dyfi industries, metal and slate mines and eventually a favourite of visitors from the English Midlands.

History shows that it has all been a matter of geography. It has been an inevitable story for a small patch of shore hemmed in by hills and marsh which was the only place on the estuary that could offer a deep safe mooring between the open sea and the tricky river to Machynlleth, the strategic centre of mid Wales. When eventually a road and a railway supplanted the Dyfi, they closely followed the same historic route along the estuary shore and created the easy access and opportunities for expanding as a resort.

The following six walks explore the village to reveal more of this history and the variety of 250 years of building. They begin in the centre where Aberdyfi began and continue chronologically to follow the development of the village as it expanded on available land up the valley and then along the coast.

(opposite) **Diagrammatic map showing the architecturally interesting and historic buildings in the centre of the village**, drawn by Liz Fenwick.

1 14 and 15 Glandyfi Terrace
2 The Medical Hall
3 Former Post Office, now Nandoras
4 Former Congregational chapel
5 Raven Hotel
6 Dovey Hotel
7 Old Custom House
8 St Peter's Church
9 Minafon and Leadenhall, 19 and 20 Seaview Terrace
10 Brynawel, 26 Seaview Terrace
11 English Presbyterian church
12 Literary Institute
13 Original Lifeboat House
14 Second Lifeboat House
15 Brynhyfryd Terrace
16 The former Tabernacle
17 13 and 14 New Street
18 12 New Street
19 Church Street cottages
20 New Street Terrace
21 Bethel Chapel
22 Imperial Hall extension
23 Former chapel
24 Imperial Hall extension
25 Liverpool House
26 8 and 9 Copper Hill Street

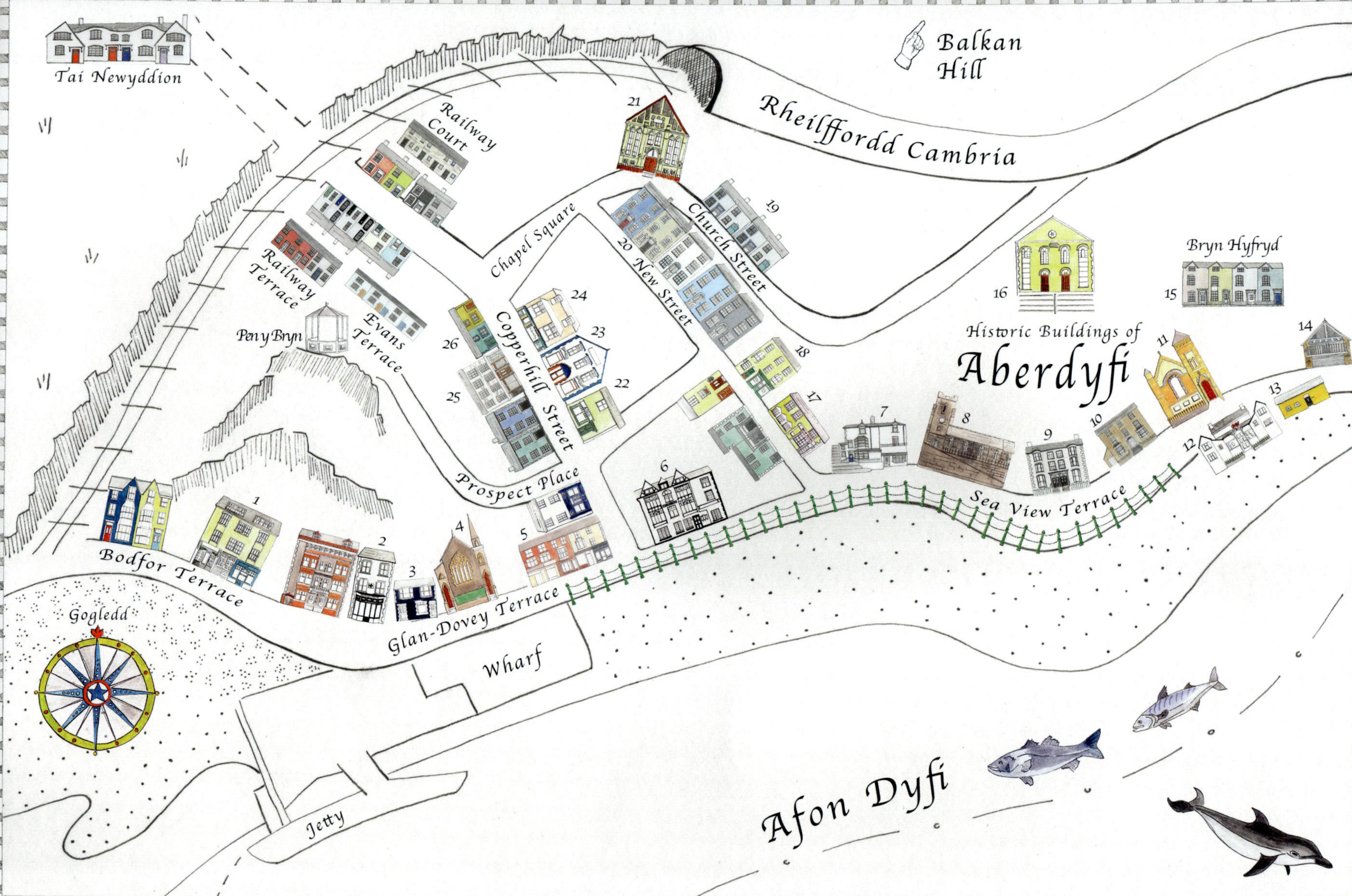

Tai Newyddion
Balkan
Hill
Rheilffordd Cambria
21
Railway
Court
Railway
Terrace
Evans
Terrace
Peny Bryn
Chapel Square
Church Street
19
20 New Street
Copperhill Street
24
23
22
26
25
Prospect Place
Bryn Hyfryd
16
15
14
18
17
Historic Buildings of
Aberdyfi
11
13
12
10
9
8
7
6
5
4
3
2
1
Bodfor Terrace
Glan-Dovey Terrace
Sea View Terrace
Gogledd
Wharf
Jetty
Afon Dyfi

Walk One

The centre, where it began

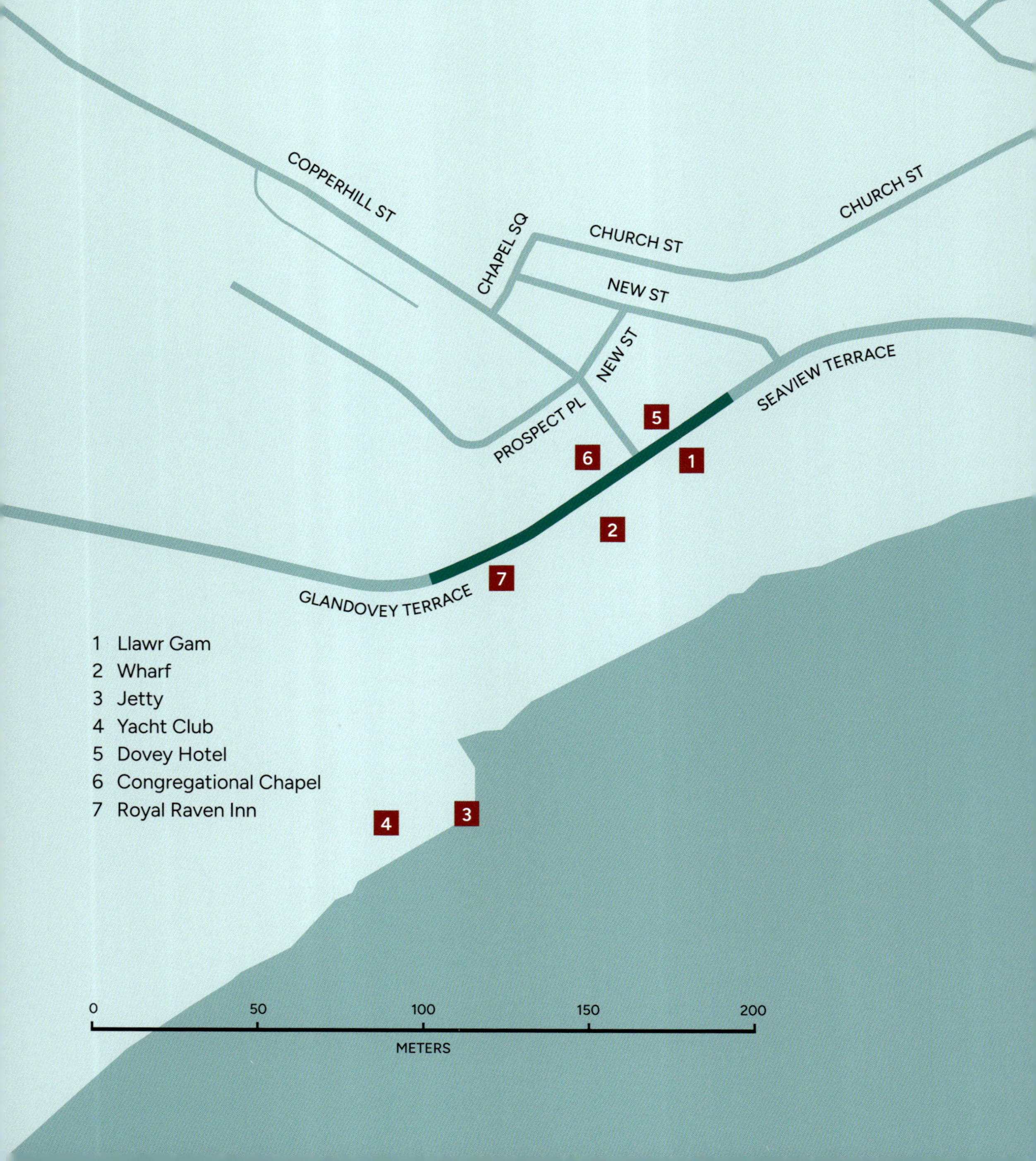

Walk One

We begin on the waterfront where Aberdyfi began as a simple mooring, close to deep water and surrounded by steep hills and marsh. This was a small area of flat shore where boats could be beached alongside at low tide, and cargoes piled nearby. Later, there were warehouses and a ferry to Ynyslas and, eventually, a village extending inland.

We are standing at **Llawr Gam** (the boatmens' seat) in front of the Dovey Hotel, where old seafarers used to congregate. Walking across the wharf to the jetty and turning around, we see the original site of the village surrounded by more recent building spreading along the shore and up and around the valley.

The **wharf** and **jetty** were built in 1885 by Abraham Williams, a local contractor who did much work for the railway, including the Mawddach viaduct. As trade prospered and declined, the wharf was altered and then fell into disuse. Eventually, the Outward Bound Trust became a Second World War tenant and the Dyfi Sailing Club began in an old air raid shelter in 1949. The wharf declined into an unsightly dump for coal, and by the time the railway was closed in 1964 the jetty and wharf were collapsing, attacked by Teredo, a timber-boring worm. After prolonged difficulties, the council was able to acquire the wharf and foreshore in 1965. Sewage disposal was improved and the wharf and jetty were rebuilt in 1972, funded by the various councils and the Outward Bound Trust.

The Pier, drawing, 1861.

Just before the construction of the railway.

Plan of wharf, *c.*1885, drawn by Liz Fenwick.

A new wharf and jetty were built on land acquired by Cambrian Railways. There were railway lines on the wharf, with turntables for wagons, and two warehouses, as well as a small store shed, a coal bunker and a shed for a rail-travelling crane. The jetty, around 370 feet, meant ships could load and unload directly to wagons whatever the tide, and that animals could walk ashore on ramps at two levels. Cattle pens and coal dumps were placed opposite what is now Glandyfi Terrace, and sand sidings provided a marshalling area in front of where Bodfor Terrace would later be built.

Aberdyfi Lifeboat Station was reopened by the RNLI in 1963 at the Outward Bound Trust boathouse. A new boathouse was built in 1991, and later an upper floor was added to provide a crew room, galley and store. In the summer there is a fund-raising shop open there.

We now see two decent replacement sheds, a visitor centre, a building for the lifeboat and the **yacht club** and a harbourmaster's office, as well as an unforgivably hideous stone toilet block. (Why has it not been rendered and painted?) The Time and Tide Bell, an art installation which hangs below the jetty, was commissioned from sculptor Marcus Vergette in July 2011. Near the top of the rising or falling tide, a gentle tolling of the bell can be heard and is a reminder of the legend of the lost land of 'Cantre'r Gwaelod'.

We return towards the Dovey Hotel. On the corner of Copper Hill Street, originally extending to an entrance to a stable yard next to London House (village stores), are the hidden remains of the former **Royal Raven Inn**, originally Tŷ Mawr.

Men and boys watching Aberdyfi regatta, *c.* 1880.

The Dyfi ferry

The ferry was ancient, perhaps as early as the twelfth century. The first written reference is in a lease to the Ynys y Maengwyn estate in 1458. By the seventeenth century there was a ferry house in a tavern known as Tŷ Mawr, later renamed the Royal Raven Inn. The ferry was especially busy from the mid eighteenth to mid nineteenth century, when harbour trade was at its peak and many mariners and shipbuilders travelled from homes in Borth. There were three ferries: Y Ferri Fawr for cattle and heavy vehicles; Y Ferri Ganol for slow traffic; Y Ferri Fach for transporting people. At low water, the ferry used a southern landing stage at Cerrig-y-Penrhyn (stone peninsula), 200 feet from Aberdyfi pier, from where poles guided passengers across the sands. At high water, the ferry ran up the River Leri to Ynyslas bridge. For many years there was a refuge on the sands for passengers caught out by the tides.

Cambrian Railways began a passenger service by paddle steamer, the Elizabeth, on the day that the railway line between Aberdyfi and Llwyngwril opened. It was not a success. *Elizabeth* frequently stuck fast on the Dyfi sandbanks, and once the new Machynlleth to Aberdyfi railway was complete, the ferry reverted to a much reduced service by the original boats.

Unloading timber at Aberdyfi wharf, John Thomas, *c.*1885.

The Royal Raven Inn, late nineteenth century.

This is hidden behind an early nineteenth-century façade and named after the crest of the Corbet family. It is almost certainly the oldest building in the village and has a beam dated 1645 within. It was probably a ferry office for some while. Part of the building was Lloft y Storehouse, a chandlers store where, for a while, an upper room housed the Calvinistic Methodists. It was converted to shops in the early twentieth century.

The Post Office and Congregational chapel, John Thomas, *c.*1885.

Aberdovey in 1834, lithograph, W. Walton.

The building to the left is the Raven Inn and the tall three-storey houses are the beginning of Seaview Terrace along the 1827 seafront turnpike. Brynhyfryd is behind. The thatched cottages in the middle, known as Tai Pen Shelf, are being demolished to make way for St Peter's Church, built in 1837. There is a beached sloop alongside a stone quay.

A family dynasty

There are around six Aberdyfi families who can trace their histories to nineteenth-century mariners, shopkeepers and business people. **William Vaughan Thomas** (1859–1931) was a prominent figure in the village. He came from Harlech and married **Elizabeth Jenkins** of Trefeddian Farm, whose father had established Aberdyfi Butchers. Together, they founded an Aberdyfi dynasty. He bought and was the founder of Medical Hall, and eventually owned four chemist shops, two in Aberdyfi (Medical Hall, and another next to the Britannia), two houses in Penhelig Terrace and other property. A founder member and first secretary of the golf club, he was influential at the Tabernacle Chapel, on the council, at the institute, and at sports and other committees. Elizabeth's relatives have remained prominent in the village, and include the Alderman **T.E. Jenkins**, butcher and redoubtable local Meirionnydd politician; **Hugh Lewis**, village historian; and his sister, **Dora Lewis**, founder of Nandoras.

Then, to the left, a row of early nineteenth-century houses, now all refronted with bay windows. The village store was known as London House after a trading destination. After a former bank building, dated 1894, by Charles F. Ellis, is the Gothic **Congregational Chapel** of 1880 which replaced a ferry office. It is in the green and grey stone which comes from Penrhyndeudraeth. It has two fine doorways – Gothic in style with flamboyant hinges – and a small bell turret. It closed in 1998 and was sensitively converted into a private house.

Next door is an early to mid nineteenth-century cottage which became the post office, originally run by a postmaster, who was also the captain of the *Elizabeth* ferry, and his two sisters. It was also the first telephone exchange. When a call or telegram was received they would whistle, and boys would compete to be paid a penny for delivery. Serious messages were taken by one of the postmistresses. In 1947, Dora Lewis and her sister-in-law, Nancy, of Cliffside, founded Nandoras clothes shop here. Dora had an excellent eye for up-to-date fashion from her training at esteemed Welsh clothes shops and Jenners in Edinburgh.

Next door is Glandyfi Medical Hall, established in 1863. Its wonderful shop front has the original lettering in the entablature and windows. From 1880 it belonged to William Vaughan Thomas.

Across Copper Hill Street is the **Dovey Hotel**, a rebuilding of the Ship Inn with a date stone: 'This house was built by Athelstan Owen Esqr, Ano Dom 1729.' What we now see is probably an early nineteenth-century rebuilding which was remodelled again by Charles F. Ellis around 1900 with fashionable new windows. Most of the rest of this section of street looks early nineteenth century. The three, at first sight rather different houses, next to the Dovey Hotel, were originally uniform with the strongly overhanging eaves carried on elegantly moulded brackets, and small-paned sash windows.

Mariners on Llawr Gam (the boatmen's seat), John Thomas, *c.*1890.

The traditional meeting place for seamen.

Walk Two

Chapel Square and Copper Hill Street

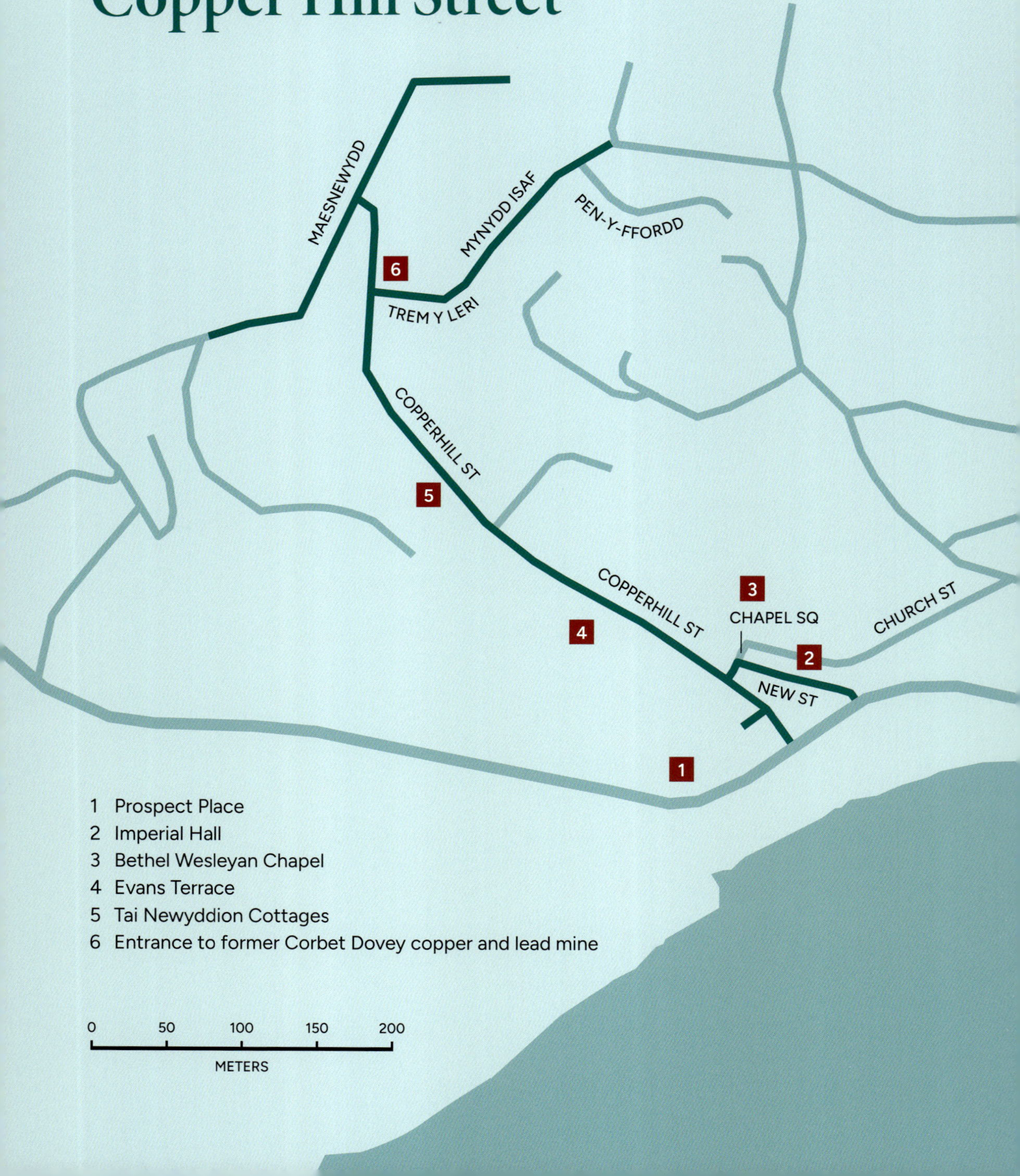

1 Prospect Place
2 Imperial Hall
3 Bethel Wesleyan Chapel
4 Evans Terrace
5 Tai Newyddion Cottages
6 Entrance to former Corbet Dovey copper and lead mine

Walk Two

Once the limited space on the shore was built up in the final years of the eighteenth century, the village developed northwards along the valley with terraces of cottages, mine workings, grander houses for merchants and sea captains, and three rival chapels. Now there is a mix of buildings, among which several buildings of probable late eighteenth century date survive, including 14 New Street, parts of the old Custom House, and perhaps some of the two-storey terrace in Copper Hill Street. The smaller houses tucked around Chapel Square (previously known as Copper Hill Square) convey a strong sense of Aberdyfi as a working port and industrial settlement. Following the construction of the railway, there was limited development of Copper Hill Street until the later twentieth-century estates on top of the former mine workings.

Beginning our walk up Copper Hill Street, we pass the handsome shop front of Aberdyfi Butchers, founded in 1861 by the Jenkins family of Trefeddian Farm.

To the west of Chapel Square is **Prospect Place**, which has a strong sense of old Aberdyfi, and is crowded with small cottages. Walking past what was the stable yard of the Royal Raven Inn, we come to the site of Capel Bach, the first Congregationalist chapel in 1845, and then of the 1894 board primary school, now converted into apartments. The former bakehouse of 1930, built to designs by Charles F. Ellis, is now a house named Ty Tŵt. Then, we walk up to Pen y Bryn, the prominent end of a north-south ridge which is now divided

Aerial view of Chapel Square, Toby Driver, RCAHMW, 2011.

Chapel Square and Copper Hill Street, *c.*1920.

Liverpool House grocers to the left with unpainted brick, chemist's shop, formerly the Victoria / then Gwalia temperance hotel, and greengrocers in Imperial Hall.

by the railway cutting. Sold by the Ynys y Maengwyn estate in 1879, it was then donated to the village. An original lookout was built on top by the council in 1897. It is claimed that this was the site of a medieval Aberdyfi castle, but a majority opinion believes this name refers to the motte-and-bailey castle still to be seen within RSPB Ynys-Hir.

Returning to Chapel Square, on the left there are three-storey buildings rendered and painted, then the mid nineteenth-century Liverpool House, unusually in painted brick. Purpose-built as a grocer's shop, it has a long front divided by fluted pilasters, and a loading door in the upper floor (now a sash window).

Numbers 8 and 9 Chapel Square are a pair of late eighteenth-century cottages. The shop across the street was formerly the Victoria, and then Gwalia, a temperance hotel. On its right-hand side there's access to the tiny and atmospheric Railway Court, presumably built in the 1860s.

Next, the most conspicuous building is **Bethel Wesleyan Chapel**, built in 1829 on land rented from Athelstan Corbet, and enlarged in 1868. It was made from brick, but rendered in 1920s. It has a plaque stating: 'BETHEL, ADDOLDY Y WESLEYAID' (Bethel, Wesleyan Place of Worship) and the dates 1829 and 1868. It has a good interior. Sadly it is now closed and its future is uncertain.

The Village Pump, John Thomas, *c.*1885.

A meeting place for women of the village, with village bakehouse Llys Awel and the Bethel Chapel behind.

Chapel Square, as laid out by Anne and Athelstan Owen of Ynys y Maengwyn, was considerably larger, but much of the space is now occupied by buildings renamed **Imperial Hall** in 1920. These were erected in 1828 as the first chapel in the village (architect, Rev. Richard Humphries), and built on a 99-year lease by the Calvinistic Methodists to replace temporary meeting places in private houses where worshippers had been persecuted by Edward Corbet.

When the growing congregation then moved to the Tabernacle in 1864, their Chapel Square building became a temporary school. The chapel was then converted and enlareged into a Market Hall and Assembly Rooms. There was a central arched passage through, with shops on the ground floor and a first-floor meeting room. From 1898, a voluntary fire brigade kept a handcart with hosepipes in a shed in the passageway, and were called out in response to a ship's foghorn. In 1931, Roman Catholics, who had no premises of their own in the village, used one of the meeting rooms. During the Second World War the building became the headquarters for the Home Guard.

Returning to the Chapel Square, New Street is a good example of an early nineteenth-century (perhaps *c.*1830) terrace of townhouses. They are rendered with three storeys at the front and two at the rear to Church Street, but do not have gardens. They are notable for preserving original sash windows and doorcases. Numbers 6 and 7, Maglona and Clifton, have attractive architraves, others have round arched doors.

Further along New Street, the gallery and the attached house have bay windows and a late nineteenth- or early twentieth-century shop front. Then, Number 14 and its neighbour, now an Indian restaurant, are surviving two-storey eighteenth-century cottages. On the corner with the waterfront is the Britannia Inn, opened in 1827 by Captain John Felix, but now with many alterations. Unusually, it is end-on to the seafront, probably meaning it is on the site of a warehouse at the bottom of New Street.

Returning again through Chapel Square, the continuation of Copper Hill Street uphill follows an old track. It starts with late eighteenth- and nineteenth-century miners' cottages. Number 14, on the east side, has a clearly nineteenth-century façade but with a date stone: 'Built by Anne Owen, 1733.' Railway Court, behind, has signs of the original limewash on tiny houses recently used for storage.

Aberdyfi schools

The first primary school, the national (or church) school, began in 1847 in the newly-vacant Calvinist Methodist chapel in the square, before moving in 1854 to a permanent home above Seaview Terrace.

In 1876, disagreements, and finally failure to agree on the appointment of a new headmaster, resulted in the Nonconformists moving to their own board school at Pen y Bryn. This cost £600 and opened in January 1894, with 102 pupils. In the Second World War evacuees used the national school, while local children went to the board school. In 1968, the two schools came together again in a new building at Penrhos. This, in turn, closed in 2013, and has been replaced by housing.

The historian **Kenneth O. Morgan** recollects in his memoir:

'The impact of that little school was so profound and valuable for me in every way... There was a warmth and security in Aberdyfi school... the facilities, I suppose were limited... but what Aberdyfi lacked in physical resources, it more than made up for in human resources. The school employed a splendid group of Welsh teachers, in one case inspirational, whose influence has remained positive and powerful upon me for the rest of my life... The absolute star of my years in Aberdyfi school was Miss Egwys Jones from Llanegryn... she inspired in me a love of learning – not only in her school subjects but in everything... she gave me the rudiments of a scholarly life because she encouraged me to pursue her subjects when I went home.'

Behind the west side of Copper Hill Street is the highly picturesque **Evans Terrace** of rendered two-storey houses with slate roofs, one of which (Number 4) bears a date stone: 'Built by Edward Price, 1827.' Numbers 3 and 5 have small-pane Yorkshire (horizontal) sashes; Numbers 3 to 6 have boarded doors. Beyond a boundary wall is the mid nineteenth-century Railway Terrace, perhaps built for railway workers, and then Bridge End cottages tucked in close to the railway bridge.

After the railway bridge the character changes. The 1860s railway curved close to the top of the then village and below most of the extensive mine workings. As soon as it was finished, houses were built along the extended Copper Hill Street.

Although there is now nothing to see, this was the site of extensive early nineteenth-century workings of the **Corbet Dovey copper and lead mine**. The mine works were to the right of Copper Hill Street, very close to Balkan House, built in 1879. There was a millpond fed by a leat from a reservoir at Y Horon above the village, a 50-foot waterwheel, a crusher and two shafts. Several other entrances or levels are known and shown on the 1902 Ordnance Survey map. There is another locked entrance at Bodfor Terrace, which originally led to a tramway directly to the estuary.

Infants at Aberdyfi Board School in Prospect Place, John Thomas, *c.*1890.

This was one of the two primary schools. In the twenty-first century the schools have closed and the now few children travel to Tywyn.

View down from Tŷ Newydd, John Thomas, *c.*1885.

This was the area of the Corbet Dovey mine. Copper Hill Street continues uphill with 1860s houses and long gardens, and then ends in a farm track. Tai Newyddion Cottages have not yet been built. On the left, at the top of the hill, is Balkan House, close to the site of the mine works.

View across Copperhill street to Balkan Hill, 1908.

Walking above the railway bridge, Lovers' Lane (with no Welsh name) on the left is a pedestrian path with a good view of the railway and several houses and runs into Bodfor Terrace. A collapse in the open hillside behind resulted in a prohibition on building. Then, a raised 1860s terrace and **Tai Newyddion Cottages** were built by the owners of Plas Penhelig for their staff, *c.*1920, in a roughcast Arts and Crafts style, the upper block having eyebrow dormers. Late Victorian Frondeg is on the right.

There has been considerable mid twentieth-century building higher up, which began at the top with Maes Newydd, a 1950s and later housing estate in typical neo-Georgian local authority style, with hipped roofs. Below, later private developments on the western slopes of Balkan Hill resulted in a number of small estates of mainly low-cost 1970s townhouses, typical of the period. Many have fine estuary views but none are of architectural note. The bungalows of Mynydd Isaf (1965) are the most conspicuous, and retain very strong period character; few places give such a strong sense of having stepped back into the 1960s and '70s. Infilling and small estates continue on the Balkan Hill hillside.

Above the village, at Y Horon, is the reservoir which supplied a leat (stream) to the Corbet Dovey mine.

Walk Three

Extending east along Seaview and Terrace Roads

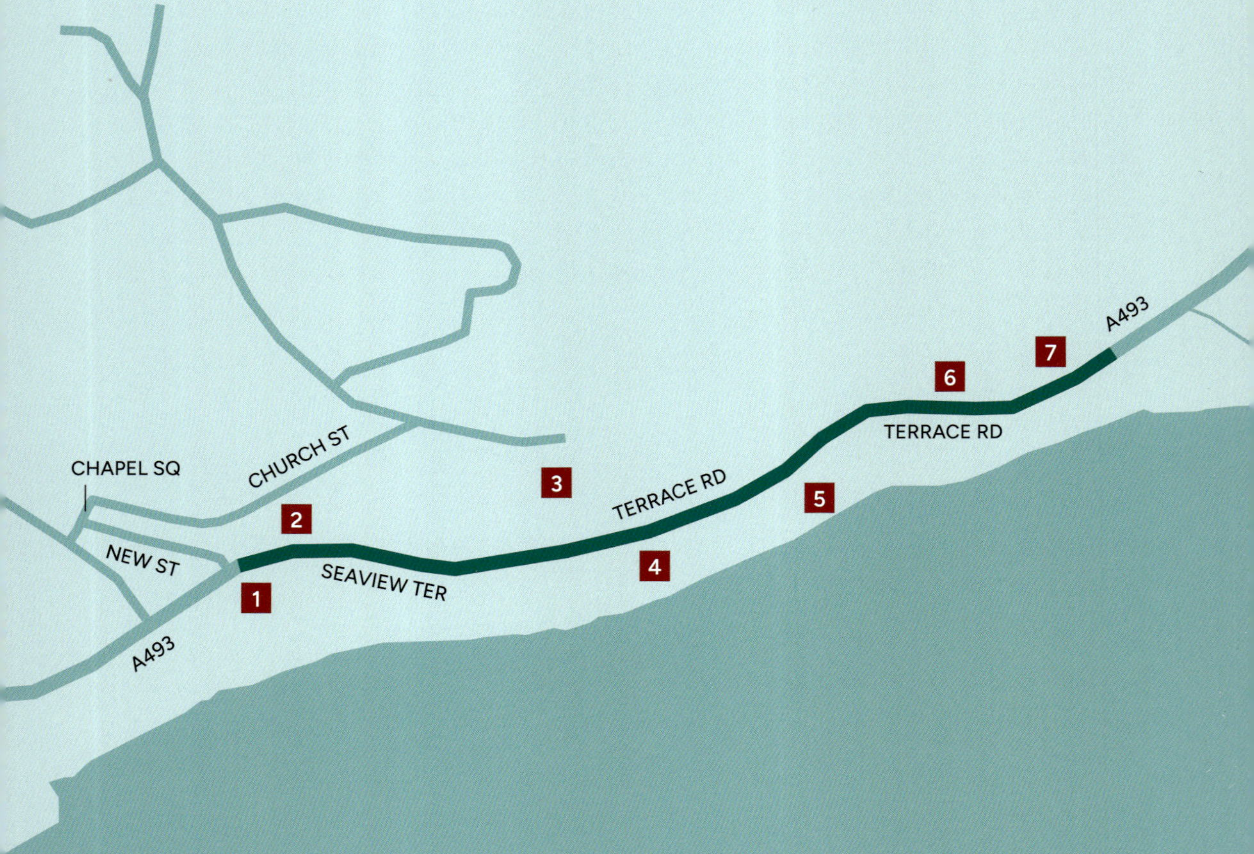

1 Custom House
2 St Peter's Church
3 National School
4 The Literary Institute
5 Lifeboat House (1859)
6 Cliffside
7 Congregational Church Hall

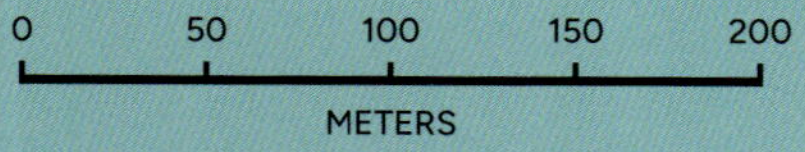

Walk Three

Seaview Terrace

The 1827 turnpike transformed an originally narrow track along a much-indented coastline to Penhelyg. It provided the opportunity to excavate and build back into the hillside and to contribute rubble to the road building. It also left small areas of land on the estuary side of the road. The 1837 Ordnance Survey and the 1841 Tithe Map show the progress of new building along the waterfront.

Across the steps, Rhiw Fach, by the side of the Brittania, is the **Old Custom House**, now though two houses with much-altered nineteenth-century façades and a large central stone chimney. It may be a rebuilding of the home of Lewis Morris, the distinguished cartographer, literary man and entrepreneur who was Customs Officer, 1751–56. On top there is a terracotta bird.

St Peter's Church was erected in 1837 on Tai Pen Shelff – a site cut into the rock and previously occupied by thatched cottages – for the benefit of residents who formerly had to walk or ride to St Cadfan's in Tywyn. The new chapel of St Peter was a so-called chapel of ease to Tywyn until Aberdyfi became a parish in its own right in 1844.

Along the roadside there are good cast iron railings and a lychgate with pretty metal leaves, of 1933, bearing the Welsh words, in gold: 'ER COF AM A. ABEL, FICER, 1931–1945,' meaning, 'In memory of A. Abel, vicar, 1931–1945.' The porch is topped by a sun

The church and Seaview Terrace, John Thomas, *c.*1895.

Aberdyfi Harbour, watercolour, Buddug Pughe, 1932.

Buddug Pughe was the daughter of Dr John Pughe of Penhelig Lodge and, later, Brynawel in Seaview Terrace. She wrote unpublished recollections of her 1860s childhood:

'In those days Aberdyfi was a real little seaport with five or six schooners, barques and brigs lying at anchor. Most of them were coastal vessels ... slates from Aberdyfi ... returning with limestone or coal. The cargoes of some of the small ships could only be landed at low tide. They discharged their cargoes opposite the church as there was then no wharf. The place was redolent of the sea, tar, ropes, pots of paint mixed with white lead. There were ships' chandlers too. Mr Robert Edwards had a shop by the Dovey, called Lloft y Storehous. The sound of caulking the sides of ships is as natural to me as 'hush-a-bye, baby' is to many a child. The sailor lads were strong and healthy – hard work at sea and good food at home. They used to walk on the quarterdeck back and fore in front of the Britannia on the Llawr Gam [meeting place by the sea], each spitting the furthest. Old John Felix, who kept the Britannia, was a most amusing old man.

'I quite vividly recollect the intense excitement that pervaded the village on the occasion of a launch. All the people in their best clothes were present, and fun and merriment were the order of the day. The ship slid into the water after the bottle had been duly smashed, and we all cheered like mad.'

dial. The village war memorial is on a wall nearby. The church is one of the few buildings of exposed stone. An initial Georgian Gothic box, it was extended in 1889 by the addition of a chancel, at a cost of £1,000. It was designed by Henry Kennedy, who dominated church architecture in the Diocese of Bangor for over 50 years. A Brindley & Foster organ was installed in 1907, and a carillon for its centenary in 1937.

The churchyard is small and mainly to the rear, with an arched entrance to Church Street. Most of gravestones date to the early and mid nineteenth century, and are of finely carved slate and inscribed in either Welsh or English with reminders of Aberdyfi's connections with the sea. After 1885, burials were at the cemetery opposite the golf course.

Inside the church's east window is a memorial to Maria Jane Pughe, Craig-y-don. She was 'an exceedingly benevolent young lady' who left £200 for schooling Aberdyfi's poor children on her death in 1872. A Gothic memorial on the north nave wall commemorates Susan Scott, who ran the girls' school in what is now Penhelig Lodge. She died 'awfully suddenly' in December 1842, aged 65, and was mourned 'by the poor in the neighbourhood'. The inscription states: 'Died in Penhelig on the XIV day December MDCCCXLII in the LXV year of her age. In testimony of their admiration of her character, gratitude for her affectionate and maternal care, this tablet is erected by some of her pupils who are sensible that they shall best perpetuate her memory by conforming their lives in her excellent example.'

There are no surviving eighteenth-century cottages along the next stretch, which has a gracious early mid nineteenth-century character. The consistency of the eaves and building line (interrupted only by the Edwardian pair) gives a very harmonious impression and suggests an element of formal planning.

Aberdovey waterfront from Craig y Penrhyn ferry landing point, lithograph, after A.F. Goddard, 1862.

The view includes a paddle steamer (perhaps the ferryboat *Elizabeth*), the church, and continuing development along the quayside.

Xanthus is a fine detached three-storey townhouse with good mid nineteenth-century detail. Immediately beyond are several pairs of three-and-a-half-storey houses, built into the hillside. Numbers 17 and 18 are good examples but numbers 19 and 20, Minafon and Leadenhall, are much the most impressive and best-preserved on the whole seafront. They are stucco with bow windows, elegant railings, steps and porches, and resemble the best similar houses Aberystwyth.

Then, Coalbrookdale iron gates, which open onto impressive slate steps up to the Tabernacle, built in 1864 to replace an earlier chapel in Chapel Square. The simple, classical, gable-fronted exterior has two inscribed tablets – one to gable reads: 'Tabernacl, Adeiladwyd 1864', and the other, lower down to centre, refers to the previous building, and reads: 'Tabernacl i'r Methodistiadd Calfinaidd yn y Flwyddyn 1828.'

Dyfi Bank and its neighbour (numbers 24 and 25) are exceptionally well-preserved Edwardian houses – beautifully detailed and quite unusual. Their two-storey bays are characteristic seaside features.

Handsome detached number 26, Brynawel, is early nineteenth century. It was originally exposed stone but now has late nineteenth-century bay windows and pebbledash. Impressive steps lead up to a very fine entrance door flanked by Doric pillars and iron railings with arrow-head finials. It was the final home of Dr John Pughe, his large family, and six servants. Alderman Jenkins, village butcher and feared local and county councillor, was a post-war resident.

The next three houses, Vanner, Celtic House and Lime House, were built by Thomas and Mary Daniel on land that Mary has been given on a nominal lease from the Ynys y Maengwyn estate where she had been a lady's maid. The Daniels lived in the now much-altered Lime House. Beyond is the yellow painted stucco English Presbyterian church (1893), designed by Richard Davies. Ellis Williams, ferry man and wartime boatman, used

Dr John Pughe

Dr John Pughe (1814–74) was a prominent and multitalented man. He qualified as a doctor at St Thomas' Hospital, London, and became one of only twelve Welsh doctors among the 850 Fellows of the Royal College of Surgeons. He spent most of his life in Aberdyfi, at Penhelig Lodge and then Brynawel. He was District Medical Officer of the Machynlleth Union, Medical Officer of Health for Tywyn, and Medical Officer for the Cambrian Railway.

He was a prominent public figure, being a Justice of the Peace and a patron of many charitable and religious causes. He was a member of the Plymouth Brethren, for whom he preached in the small church which he established at the Bath House, Aberdyfi (now the Literary Institute), and was an accomplished Cymric scholar. He was buried in a family vault at Cwm Maethlon chapel. Four sons were physicians, and his daughter, Buddug Pughe (1857–1939), was a professional Welsh artist who wrote a history of her native district.

The old lifeboat house with Cliffside and Mervinia Terrace behind, John Thomas, *c.*1890.

The first lifeboat, *The Victoria*, was provided by the harbour authorities and housed in the building standing in the water on Terrace Road. The boat had to be taken out of the west end and wheeled down the road to a slipway. The lifeboat was taken over by the RNLI in 1853, which bought a new site for £150 and built a new lifeboat house at a cost of £320. It was enlarged in 1886, and in 1903 the slipway was built opposite. The lifeboat house closed in 1931 but reopened in 1963 on the wharf at the Outward Bound warehouse, until the present house was built next to the wharf.

to sit with his telescope in the front room of number 31 checking whether there were passengers waiting or stranded on the refuge.

A zig-zag path leads up to the former **national (or church) school** built in 1854 to replace its first (1847) temporary accommodation in Chapel Square.

Opposite, on the estuary side, the **Literary Institute** was, from the 1840s, a chapel for a sect of the Plymouth Brethren. It became vacant in 1882 at a time when there was local interest in national proposals for science and art classes in remote areas. As it was ideally sited, the lease was acquired for a new institute within two days of an inaugural meeting. The 1897 veranda was donated by John Corbett, and Capel Baddon Baptist Chapel, built in 1901, was incorporated. Charles F. Ellis designed some further alterations in the 1920s/1930s. The anchor in the forecourt was discovered in the estuary, and may have been associated with a ferry. Recent conversions of the side wings have resulted in inappropriate modern windows and intrusive illuminated advertisements.

Cliffside, with the two lifeboat houses and Gray Jones garage, John Thomas, *c.*1885.

The institute became a focal point for many village organisations, as it held lectures, chess and draughts too. There were newspapers and reference books to read, with the most popular periodical being the *Shipping Gazette*. Downstairs, there was a billiard room and a members-only terrace, where the former place of baptisms is now marked by a grid. It is a rare survivor of the once common public reading rooms.

Bath Place, presumably built on a spur of land, is next door, and includes the two-storey three-bay Plas Dyfi and two neighbouring single-storey houses, perhaps originally for fishermen.

Terrace Road

Seaview Terrace then becomes Terrace Road, with mainly later nineteenth- and twentieth-century houses and cottages – and a more fragmented development pattern than Seaview Terrace. Set above on the hillside, accessible only on foot, is Brynhyfryd Terrace – four early nineteenth-century houses (clearly visible on the 1834 print). They are two storeys plus an attic, rendered and with slate roofs. Two have elegant doorcases. The Rev. D.W. Morgan, author of *Brief Glory*, the history of the Dyfi shipping, lived here. Very close behind is another simpler terrace of similar date.

On the estuary side of Terrace Road is the original lifeboat house of 1837, with plaques (now hidden behind a hedge) on a wall. After Glanaber, early nineteenth century, the street line is broken by the rather odd, late twentieth-century stepped houses with car parking which replaced Gray Jones, for many years the village garage. Further along is the 1859 and later **lifeboat house** . It is now a house with garages below and full width windows above.

Next door, a pair of houses in industrial redbrick, Neuadd and Exchange, the latter once the site of the telephone exchange and then of wartime accommodation for the Outward Bound Trust. Next door is 5 Terrace Road, an early cottage, which very regrettably no longer has its original ground-floor sash window.

Almost opposite, standing in the water on the estuary side of road, is Glanydon, built by shipbuilder Roger Lewis so that his ships could unload directly. Now a terrace of four houses – three of which have lost much of their character, with the stained pebbledash and crude modern windows.

1 to 4 **Cliffside** is a terrace of four stuccoed houses. In 1877, Margaret Thomas, wife of the Medical Hall chemist, bought the site of a defunct lime kiln and built these houses for her four children. Her daughter Sarah married Hugh Lewis of Llanegryn in 1900, and set up home in 4 Cliffside. Their children included Dora (founder of Nandoras) and Hugh (councillor, and prolific local history author) who lived their whole lives there. The houses have Gothic decoration applied to an otherwise fairly conventional house plan, with the ubiquitous seaside bay windows. The brilliant white paint makes it difficult to see the quality of the most elegant stucco decoration and of the good iron railings.

Just behind, reached by steps, is Mervinia Terrace, a well-preserved simple mid nineteenth-century terrace of four two-storey cottages for seafarers, grouped as two mirrored pairs, rendered, with slate roofs. They are slightly lower status than Brynhyfryd Terrace.

Opposite is the former Arts and Crafts and roughcast **Congregational Church Hall** (1922), which is now an attractive private house with a terrace to the estuary. Beyond the adjacent semi-detached cottages are lock-up garages on the site of the former smithy, once a favoured meeting place for men and boys.

There is a concrete basin in the river, which was used by salmon fishermen who, in winter, gathered mussels using eighteen-foot rakes and then put them in the basin to be washed in sacks for 48 hours.

Above is an attractive path to Penhelyg, which runs on the hillside above the waterside buildings. It has a mix of both formally planted and self-seeded vegetation, with views across the estuary.

Walk Four

Penhelyg and beyond

1 Slate mines
2 Nantiesyn
3 Plas Penhelig
4 Penhelig Lodge
5 Penhelig Park
6 Roman Road (Hen Ffordd Corbet Road)
7 Coed y Glyn
8 Outward Bound Trust

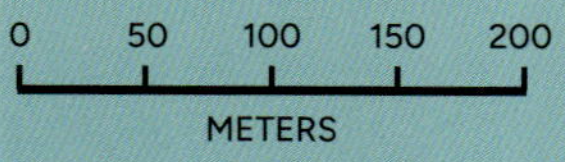

Walk Four

Penhelyg was originally a separate tiny fishing hamlet, on an inlet at the bottom of a narrow valley with a stream, with its own sheltered microclimate. It was much altered by **slate mining** and shipbuilding, and in the 1860s it was totally changed by the building of the railway embankment across its harbour, and the deposit of tunnel spoil. Buddug Pughe, the artist who was born at Penhelig Lodge, recalled: 'The next event I remember is the coming of the railway. People were much disturbed by this. We children listened to the talk of our elders, mostly servants, and grew more terrified each day. The operations going on preparatory to its arrival were tremendous and upheaving. The solid rock was blasted with shattering noises; fragments of rock were then hurled into our dear little cove, completely blocking it up until our house grew darker each week as the hideous embankment grew higher and higher.'

Walking from Aberdyfi, the view is dominated by Penhelig Terrace and the railway embankment. The three-storey Penhelig Arms is on the left. Shown on 1837 and 1841 maps, its core is early nineteenth century, built by Captain Humphrey Edwards, a retired master mariner – but the left side is modern. It overlooks a small harbour with an ever-more skeletal wood breakwater. Looking ahead, the road gives an indication of the former shoreline.

Penhelig from the old road to Aberdiffi, pencil drawing, Miss Browning, 1821.

The narrow winding track from Aberdyfi to Penhelyg is cut into the hillside. The oldest stone building (later Mrs Scott's school, and then the home of Dr John Pughe and Penhelig Lodge) and shipbuilding yards are on the far side of the harbour. The Corbet Road, of around 1808, is at estuary level.

Penhelig View, drawing, unknown artist, 1837.

The 1827 turnpike can be seen descending on the hillside into Penhelyg and then along the waterfront as a widened road.

Opposite the Penhelig Arms, a path leads past the site of a shipbuilding yard to the typically Victorian Penhelig Terrace. Built in stages from 1898 on tunnel spoil deposited in 1860s, its houses were designed by Charles F. Ellis and were sold with difficulty over several years. It looks as if each original standard unit was slightly differently customised by the original occupants or builders over a prolonged period, and that alterations have continued, so that they are now all quite individual. They are two-and-a-half-storey houses and, compared with the more central houses, they have quite spacious layouts – wide double frontages and long front gardens to the water (and car parking).

Back along the main road there is a terrace of tall multi-coloured pebble-dashed houses, *c.*1860, and similar to many on Aberdyfi seafront, but with no views and therefore no bay windows. The corner house to **Nantiesyn** was once the local Penhelyg shop.

Above the railway bridge is the Penhelyg railway halt, built in 1933 with a pagoda waiting room (one of only two in Wales) in response to public demand for a more convenient station. In the Second World War it was staffed by Dora and Nancy Lewis of Cliffside and Nandoras, but is now a request stop.

Nantiesyn is a characterful rendered terrace, probably begun in the mid nineteenth century and then growing piecemeal. At the lower end are two-storey houses with dormers, rendered, many with sash windows. Further uphill are later houses with bay windows;

Penhelyg harbour, watercolour, C. Cook, *c.*1910.

The breakwater can be seen in its original state.

three houses near the top are late twentieth century. Tŷ Coch, 9 Nantiesyn, was the first home of Nonconformists in the village.

Above Nantiesyn, at Allt Goch, there are three entrances to mid nineteenth-century slate mines, with several large caverns. Little is known of their operation. Also above Nantiesyn, and conspicuous from the road approach to the village, is the substantial former vicarage built by the time of the 1889 map. It is now Plas y Coed, and was earlier the home of Dr Tibbott Davies (Dr Tom), the village doctor and prominent local personality for 30 years after the Second World War. He combined a single-handed rural general practice far from hospitals with passions for wildfowling, rough-shooting and fly-fishing.

Plas Penhelig was built in 1908 by brothers David and Joseph Mathew Howells – a prominent local family who made fortunes through investment in south Wales coal mines and shipping. The family lived in considerable style, remote from everyday village life, in the very substantial house with outbuildings and glasshouses and large hillside gardens. There were seven live-in staff and five gardeners. The coachman, the head gardener and another staff member lived in the three houses of Penhelig Lodge at the bottom of the drive, and seven staff houses were built along Copper Hill Street.

The family were enthusiastic members of the golf club. Plas Penhelig was inherited by a niece, Alison Rieben, who was Welsh ladies' golf amateur champion in 1929 and

1936, and president of the Aberdyfi club in 1962. Her daughter Isabella was Welsh ladies' amateur golf champion in 1932, 1949 and 1951. When Mrs Rieben died in 1974, her five grandchildren sold Plas Penhelig and it became a hotel, eventually reverting to a private house. Its impressive hillside gardens benefit from a sheltered microclimate. The lower part of the gardens, partly visible from the car park, is now separately owned and based on restored ancient woodland, and splendidly planted with bulbs and shrubs.

At the foot of the drive, and overlooked by Nantiesyn Terrace, is a car park built on land donated by the Rieben family in 1978. The stream is now in a culvert which runs under the roundabout and empties into the estuary opposite the Penhelig Arms.

After the modern car park is the oldest surviving building in Penhelyg, **Penhelig Lodge**. Originally by the waterside, it is now three early nineteenth-century houses of rubble stone with a rendered ground-floor. From around 1820 to 1842, and as a single house, it was a boarding school for young ladies, and owned by Mrs Susan Scott, who is remembered fondly in the church. The fees were £100 a year, with teaching by Mrs Scott, her sister Miss Strong, and foreign governesses. It was then, for 19 years from 1844, the home with seven acres of Dr John Pughe. Later it was the lodge to the new Plas Penhelig.

Below the railway is **Penhelig Park**, monument and garden, laid out on the site of a shipyard, with the Commando memorial and seawall plaque remembering 3 Troop, No. 10 (Inter-Allied) Commando. This was a remarkable secret group of 86 German-speaking,

Shipbuilding

The growth of industry and trade resulted in a busy and successful shipbuilding industry around the Dyfi estuary between 1761 and 1880. It was made easier by the 1786 Shipping Act, which encouraged local shipbuilding by enabling shared ownership by small investors. New ships were financed by dividing the overall building costs into 64 shares, which were made available for sale to a maximum of 32 people. The owners were usually consortia of farmers, timber merchants, local entrepreneurs and mariners. Ships could be built in any convenient space by the water's edge where there was a supply of timber, a sawpit and a boiler to make the planks pliable enough to fit to the frames. There were no plans, only half-hull models carved by the shipwright, who then supervised the building of several ships at once by organising local craftsmen.

The first recorded ship was the *Nelly*, built at Derwenlas in 1761, and the first at Aberdyfi was the *Linnet*, built in 1769 at a yard opposite Penhelig Lodge. In the early years most shipbuilding was around Derwenlas, but in the peak period for slate exports, boats became larger – principally, schooners – and most were built at Aberdyfi yards. At least 60 ships were built on the Dyfi between 1840 and 1880.

There were five yards at Penhelyg and along the shore towards and beyond Bryn Llestair (Picnic Island), and another on the site of Bodfor Terrace.

View over Penhelyg Rock, John Thomas, *c.*1890.

The railway embankment has been cut across the Penhelyg inlet, reducing the size of the harbour and obliterating shipbuilding yards. The Penhelig Arms looks over the largely filled-in harbour where tunnel spoil has been spread. There was doubt about how stable it would be for building houses, but eventually Penhelig Terrace was erected from 1898.

mainly Jewish, refugees who were billeted in Aberdyfi family homes during 1942 and 1943. They were given fictitious names and trained for special duties in commando skills, reconnaissance, interrogation and intelligence. Deployed singly or in small groups, they played distinguished roles in Italy and after the Normandy landings. Twenty were killed in action; three married local girls.

The monument, which was unveiled in 1999 in the presence of 28 survivors, reads: 'For the members of 3 Troop 10 (IA) Commando who were warmly welcomed in Aberdyfi while training for special duties in battle, 1942–43. Twenty were killed in action.'

Beyond, we can walk onto the Hen Ffordd Corbet Road, a shelf of rock just above the tidal level, and popularly known as the **Roman Road**. It was Edward Corbet of the Ynys y Maengwyn estate's attempt, in around 1808, to get his metal ore and other goods to ships at the River Dyfi's mouth. His plan was for the road to stretch the length of his land, from Pennal down the River Dyfi, just above the high tide level, and along the four miles of beach to Tywyn. It required blasting through rock, and he is said to have employed ex-servicemen from Wellington's army. However, it failed, as the road began to collapse into the estuary even as it was being built. Much of the road was destroyed by the building of the railway, but stretches can be seen along the estuary shore.

View east from Penhelyg harbour, with tunnel spoil, railway embankment and houses along the hillside main road.

After the railway bridge, the road climbs with a mixture of nineteenth- and twentieth-century houses and cottages on the left, which presumably relate to the working history of Penhelyg. On the right, there is a tremendous view of the harbour and village. Most notable are:

- Maybank House, 4 Plas Meirion, Penhelyg Road, built *c.*1865 by Thomas Ellis, a builder working for the Cambrian Railway company. It was here that his son Charles and daughter Lizzie grew up. Charles F. Ellis, the local architect, lived in Maybank for most of the rest of his life.
- The Cottage, 20 Penhelyg Road, an early cottage.
- Copper Cottage, the stone-built former police station.
- Tanyrallt, a very nice example of a late Georgian house – lovely symmetrical planning and nice use of stone.

Then, higher up on the hillside is Philip Avenue. It has terrific views and is a line of early 1930s houses, situated on land sold by Mrs B.A. Hunt to Harry and Rachel Joyce of Birmingham, and named after their son Philip who was shot down while serving in the Royal Flying Corps in 1917. The layout of the road and most (probably all) of the houses were built to designs by Charles F. Ellis. They are a good sequence of domestic architecture in a variety of styles, including Tawelfan, which has Art Deco wrap-around Crittall windows. Many have been modified in recent years, but original features included in the architectural plans remain.

At the far end, not easily seen, is the Joyce family home itself, the Arts and Crafts **Coed y Glyn** (1934), again by Charles F. Ellis, which has a very good 4½-acre garden and its own a drive to the main road. It is one the best Aberdyfi houses – stylistically difficult to classify, as it has some elements of Arts and Crafts (materials, big roofs, asymmetry, leaded light windows) but is mainly a very stylish 1930s modern house with clean lines and a disciplined façade with the strong geometry of its veranda and wide windows. There is a pleasing contrast between its roughcast walls and the small stone of the garden walls.

Next door, on the main road, is the principal building of the **Outward Bound Trust**, the uninspired late nineteenth-century Bryn Eithin, which is surrounded by modern outbuildings.

Nantiesyn, John Thomas, *c.*1885.

The Penhelyg village shop is opposite the stream and undergrowth which is nowadays a car park. The vicarage is above.

Bryn Llestair (Picnic Island) is an outcrop of rock and viewpoint, cut off by a railway cutting.

Next, invisible above the road, and up a long track, is Trefri Fawr, a characterful farmhouse, probably seventeenth and eighteenth century with later additions, and a detached barn, partly built into a slope of grey-brown rubble, with a slate roof and the date stone: 'Elinor Jones, John Jones, 1738.' There are records of farming on the site going back to the thirteenth century.

A cavern in the Penhelyg slate mines, © Roy Fellows

There are enticing views of Plas Trefri from the road, the hillside and the estuary. Thought to date back to humble beginnings as a fisherman's hovel, the prominent hall was built in 1835 for Robert Griffiths of Bishop's Castle, who was one of the commissioners for the enclosure and drainage of Cors Fochno. It has a stone ground-floor and is roughcast above. It is set in impressive gardens, including a castellated stone fort on a small island.

Further on, Braich y Celyn Hall is above the road. There is also a lodge and an overgrown walled garden. The hall began life in the sixteenth century or later as a farmhouse. During the eighteenth century, a large extension and a third floor was added. Then, in Victorian times, it was extended with a third wing and a coach house. Unlisted, it has suffered unsympathetic alterations.

Beyond, towards the edge of the parish, is the hamlet of Abertafol, once the site of a waterside tannery and a winter harbour. On the hillside above, where paths lead to Llyn Barfog, is Tafolgraig, a seventeenth-century and later listed farmhouse and barn. On the headland below the sharp bend in the road is a house built in 1940 by the engineer responsible for wartime beach defences. He made full use of war department men and materials.

Further on is Plas Panteidal, with the remains of lead mines. It was the summer residence, from 1900, of Bishop Watkin Williams of Bangor, to which he retired and

Shipbuilding at Aberdyfi, watercolour, Harriette Brooke, 1850s.

A ship is under construction close to what became Bryn Llestair (Picnic Island), with Trefri beyond, while horses appear to drag logs along the shore. Hen Ffordd Corbet (*c.*1808) is on the left.

lived with large staff until his death in 1944. Soon after, the house was destroyed by fire. The stables survive and are now surrounded by conifer forest and chalets. The lodge cottage by the road was briefly the home, in the late 1950s, of prolific romantic novelist Countess Barcynska (also Mrs Caradoc Evans, etc.) who claimed healing powers for her miracle stone.

Finally there is Frongoch, an elaborate quarry, adjacent to a river wharf which opened in around 1870. In 1884, a harsh frost shattered the large mounds of slates, and quarrying never recovered. It is now known, on uncertain authority, as Smugglers' Cove boatyard.

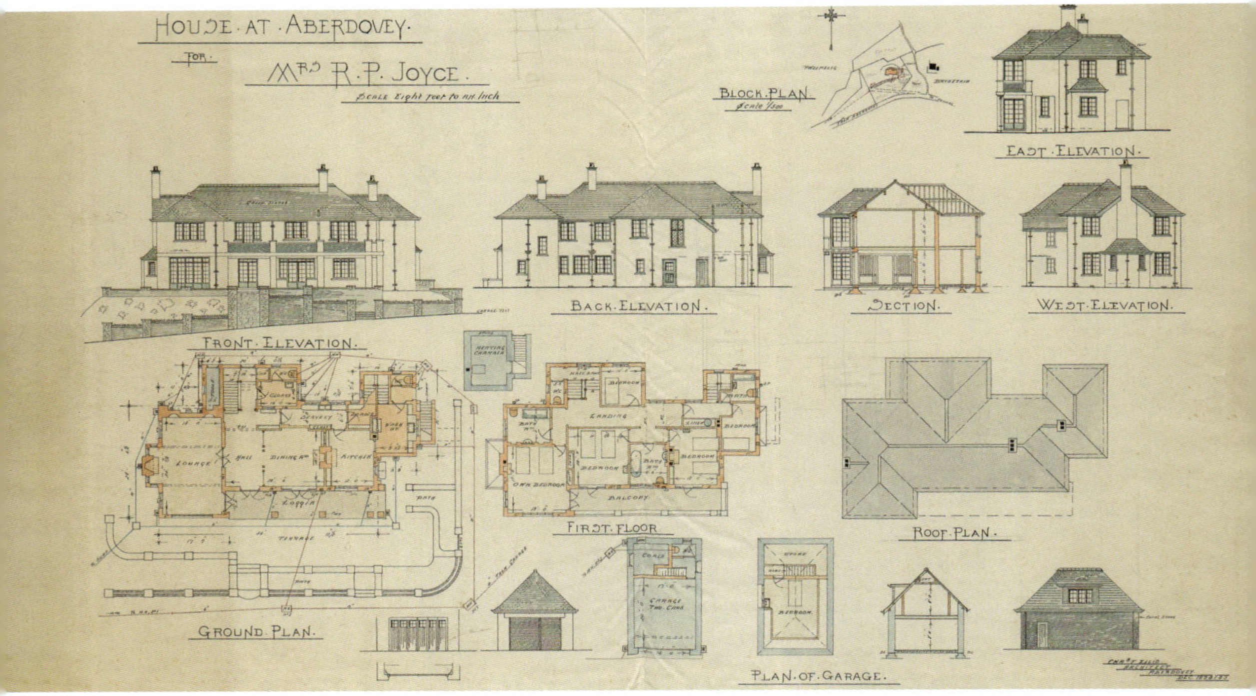

Coed y Glyn, Philip Avenue, drawing by Charles F. Ellis, 1934.

Outward Bound Trust

Established in 1941 by **Kurt Hahn**, the founder of Gordonstoun School, and by **Lawrence Holt**, senior partner of his family's Blue Funnel Shipping Line. Its purpose was to train young seamen in small boat skills so as to improve their survival chances if their ships were torpedoed in the mid-Atlantic. **Capt. J.F. 'Freddie' Fuller**, who took charge in 1942, had himself survived two torpedo attacks and commanded an open lifeboat in the Atlantic Ocean for 35 days. What began as training for resilience at sea quickly became a broader model for cultivating courage, compassion, teamwork, and service. Now run by an educational charity, the Outward Bound Trust was established in 1946. Initially it provided military-style courses of 26 days for cadets, schoolboys, borstal boys and companies. More recently, courses have become shorter and mainly for schools. Girls were initially housed at Rhowniar, but are now equal in numbers on the main site.

In the earlier years, Outward Bound instructors were closely involved with the Aberdyfi lifeboat, housed in their wharf shed, and they still contribute.

Aberdyfi Search and Rescue Team was formally founded in 1973 by Outward Bound instructors, but became an independent group operating within an umbrella national voluntary organisation, with well-defined training and protocols. It has around 45 members, with a vehicle at the Outward Bound centre and another at Dolgellau, and collaborates with helicopters. They have an impressive record.

Walk Five

Up Church Street to Balkan Hill

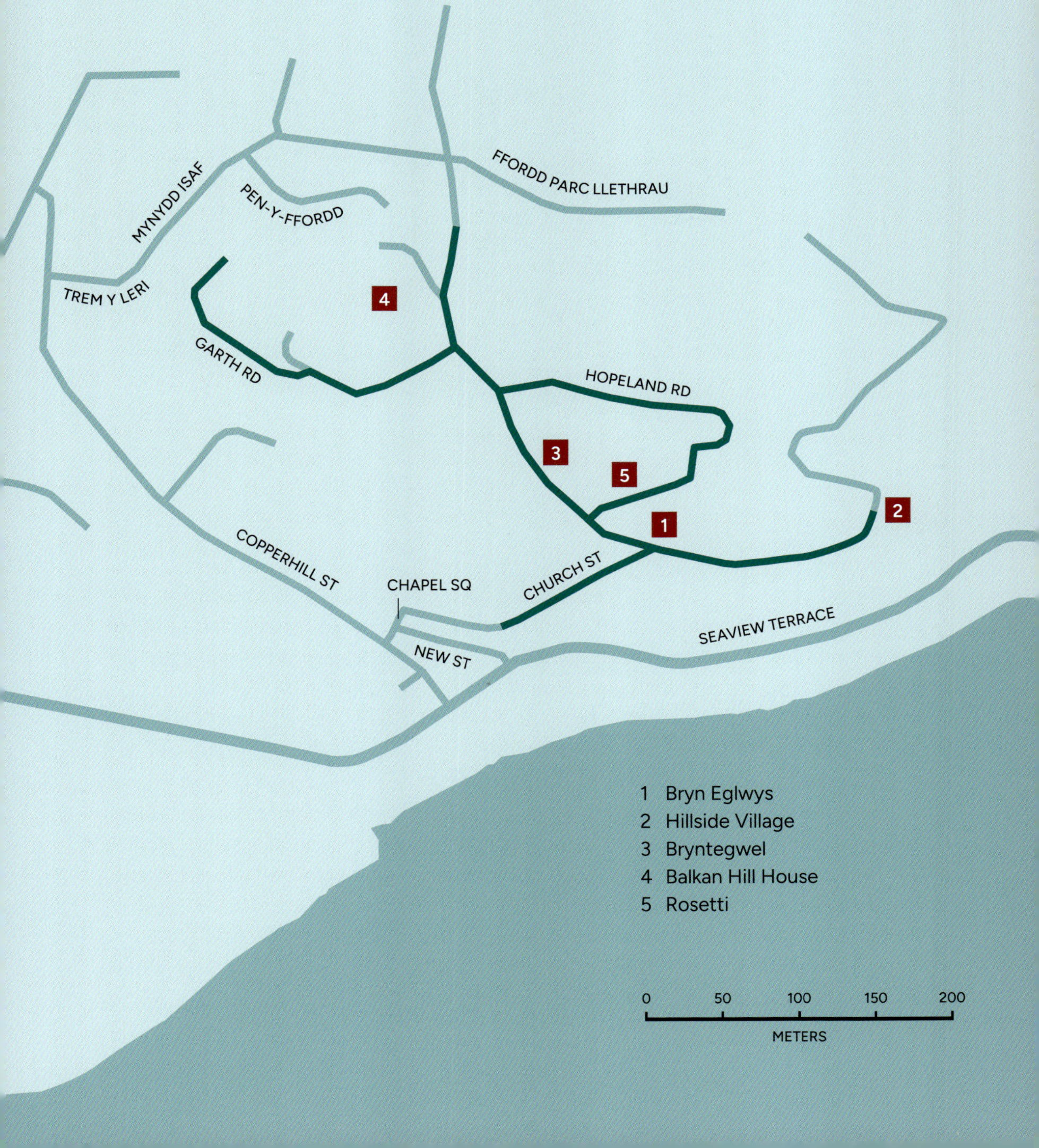

1 Bryn Eglwys
2 Hillside Village
3 Bryntegwel
4 Balkan Hill House
5 Rosetti

Ordnance Survey, 1: 2500, 1974.

Section to show Balkan Hill. Buildings mentioned in the text are coloured red.

Walk Five

Church Street began as an ancient track leading up to the hills and Cwm Maethlon, with cottages on its lower left side as Chapel Square became built up. In the last quarter of the nineteenth century, large plots higher up the hill began to be developed for much grander houses with sea views and ornamental gardens.

On the right are the backs of New Street houses which do not have gardens. They were built on the slope so that their rear access is to their upper storeys. Beyond is a handsome churchyard gate, and recent infill in the steep gardens of Seaview Terrace houses. On the other side of the road, the early nineteenth-century cottages, with Gibraltar Terrace behind, are still full of character. Near the bottom of the hill there was once a cobbler's shop. Higher up, the houses are larger with better views and more air, beginning with Fairview House, built to a 1905 design by Charles F. Ellis.

Building on what became known as Balkan Hill began after the final sales of lots by the Ynys y Maengwyn estate in the 1870s. Soon, a demand for larger detached houses with gardens and views was met by sales by the new landowners to private buyers and builder/developers.

John Madin and Hillside Village

In 1967, **John Madin** (1924–2012), a successful and respected Birmingham architect and controversial town planner, bought 29 acres on Balkan Hill, and obtained permission for 401 holiday houses, of which 41 were built, including Eastwards and Westwards, a pair for Madin himself.

'I have been doing this since 1967,' he explained. 'About a year before that I was looking for somewhere by the sea, but near to Birmingham, where I lived, to have a holiday home. A friend of mine had a light plane and he flew us up and down the Welsh coast and I chose Aberdovey from the air... I bought the land because I was very anxious that this beautiful village not be spoilt by speculative development, as so many other seaside towns along the coast had been. At that time I was designing Telford new town. The chairman of the planning committee at Aberdovey said why didn't I do a plan for the development and extension of the village. I agreed to do that, and I have been slowly developing it ever since.'

There was always local concern about the disproportionate scale of the proposed development and its demands on public services. In 2022, the Supreme Court supported Snowdonia National Park in quashing the original permission. It ruled that the developer could not rely on a 1967 planning permission to build 401 houses because the subsequent development of 41 houses under different, later permissions, made it impossible to complete the original scheme.

Along the level section of Church Street is **Bryn Eglwys**, a nineteenth-century stone-built property, altered in the early twentieth century to designs by Charles F. Ellis. It is an interesting contrast with its earlier neighbours, built in the Georgian tradition, but having quite a different feel, with roughcast render superseding stucco. In recent years, there has been more modest infill, the substantial and controversial **Hillside Village** (1967 and later) with houses and flats in pairs, and short terraces following the contours of the hillside.

Balkan Hill doubles back along the line of the old track, with detached Victorian villas, originally set in large gardens, positioned to make the most of the views.

- Bryn Dyfi and coach house, on the corner, is perhaps the earliest house and is shown on the 1841 Tithe Map.
- **Bryntegwel** is a substantial Victorian house in two-acre gardens, originally the holiday home of bachelor Eton master C. H. Allcock, who used to entertain mid-winter relays of schoolmaster golfers. Bernard Darwin would join them for a week, and described a routine of two-and-a-half rounds of golf, tea, bridge and billiards, and dinner. A lovely, lively picturesque composition, Bryntegwel is so unlike the solid Georgian symmetry of earlier houses; it is now divided into flats.

Section of an 1863 map of Aberdyfi. It shows the suggested line of the Cambrian railway deviation, immediately behind the village. The mine works are at the top, close to the present Balkan Hill road.

The map shows the whole village, with very little building on Terrace Road, Bodfor Terrace or upper Church Street. The Raven and Ship (Dovey) Inns are connected.

- Bryn Derw.
- **Balkan Hill House** was built on a seven-acre plot above the former mine works which were sold, in 1879, to Captain John Lewis, a retired master mariner and ship owner. It is characterised by asymmetry and multiple gables and had gardens in the shape of a ship's hull, now much reduced by division into small plots.

Close by, there are a number of less showy Edwardian villas built as private residences. There has also been more recent infill. Nearby, in Garth Road, a narrow cul-de-sac, are Preswylfa, Brynarfor, Argoed and Brynawelon, large houses with substantial gardens and characterised by multiple gables and relatively steeply pitched roofs with red ridge tiles and redbrick chimneys. Brynawelon is by Clough Williams-Ellis.

Aerial view of Balkan Hill and Hopeland Road, © Glyn Davies.

Hopeland Road seems to be the first more ambitious planned development of a group of houses, slightly later than Balkan Hill but shown on the 1902 Ordnance Survey map. The original layout is intact, with typical late Victorian villas in a variety of styles. Most have rendered painted walls, usually white, with large gabled dormers, half-timber decoration, verandas, and large amounts of varied glazing. They are set in a landscape of planned gardens with a good many trees, separated by large privet hedges and striking boundary walls of the small, thin local stone. The artist Buddug Pughe lived from 1905 to 1939 in a house with the best view that she named **Rosetti** after a favourite painter.

Beyond Balkan Hill the road continues to the hilltop where, looking back, the reservoir of Y Horon is prominent. Then, along the Panorama Walk with wonderful views, one eventually comes to Bwlch farmhouse. Beyond, a track runs past Llyn Barfog to Pennal.

Walk Six

Extending west: Glandyfi and Bodfor Terraces and the western approach

1 14 and 15 Glandyfi Terrace
2 Corbet Dovey mine
3 Craig y Don
4 Neuadd Dyfi
5 Gwelfor Road
6 Railway Station

Walk Six

The first developments to the west were an entrance and tramway for the Corbet Dovey mine in around 1800, and a boatyard nearby in mid-century. Railway sidings in the sand followed in the 1860s. Apart from the first few houses, begun shortly after the turnpike, housing development to the railway bridge was later than Seaview Terrace, but largely complete by the time of the 1889 Ordnance Survey map. This side of the village seems to have always had a resort character to it, in contrast to the earlier Seaview Terrace, which looks much more like gracious private dwellings. The continuous line of terraced boarding houses along Bodfor Terrace resembles seaside resorts throughout the length of Britain. Beyond the railway bridge are large early twentieth-century hillside houses, and unplanned and undistinguished developments up to the railway station and golf course.

Beginning opposite the wharf, Westhaven, 17 Glandyfi Terrace, is a bombastic dark red-stone pair of lodging houses with square bays and elaborate white painted metalwork. As the Harbour Hotel, it was the wartime home for Gordonstoun School, and is now apartments.

14 and 15 Glandyfi Terrace are a particularly handsome pair of early nineteenth-century stucco houses, with early twentieth-century shop fronts. They are three storeys plus attics, and have very elegant two-storey bow windows on the first and second floors.

View of Bodfor Terrace with the railway sidings, early twentieth century.

The road has now been widened, and there is a new lower wall and a large car park. The terraces are shown here in a largely unaltered state.

In the centre of the ground-floor are steps up to recessed porches with Doric columns.

The rest of Glandyfi Terrace and Bodfor Terrace were built in several short terraces. They are in a mixture of styles and decoration, some having columns on the bay windows, and round door arches, while others have doors which are square-headed with bracketed cornices. While there is pictorial evidence that, originally, the terraces were uniform without bay windows, nearly all the houses have now been rebuilt to a relatively standard height of three storeys with attics, and nearly all have bays, and many are greatly altered with changed bays, dormers and decoration. There are a number of early and later twentieth-century shop fronts.

Opposite the terraces, there was originally a five-foot wall along the 1827 turnpike road, which partially hid railway sidings in the sand. In 1970, this area was transformed when the wall was removed, the road widened, and the car park built.

The historian Kenneth Morgan (later Vice-Chancellor of UCW, Aberystwyth and Lord Morgan of Aberdyfi) spent his wartime childhhod at Number 11 Bodfor Terrace, his grandmother's lodging house. An alley between numbers 8 and 9 leads to an area where the blocked entrance of the **Corbet Dovey mine** can be seen in the cliff side. A tramway led directly from the mine across the sand to ships. Number 9, Pomona, was the home of Berta Ruck.

At the very end – the 1970 fire station, and immediately beyond Bodfor Terrace – the railway divides the village with a deep cutting through a north-south ridge behind the houses, and a 1860s bridge across the main road (with a 1990 tunnel). The low-lying land behind the sand dunes beyond was originally marsh and liable to frequent flooding, but this was changed by the railway embankment and by drainage. The path under the railway, with a recent wildlife hedge, is known as the Burma Road after the wartime supply route.

There were only two significant buildings before the arrival of the railway, the Corbet Arms and **Craig y Don**. Then came the golf course and, in the early twentieth century, the Penrhos hillside became desirable as a site for villas with gardens and sea views. A little later, the low ground was developed for recreation, and most recently for a sprawl of housing and mobile homes.

Berta Ruck

Berta Ruck (1878–1978) was, for the last 40 of her 100 years, a distinguished and flamboyant Aberdyfi resident, and was related to Lord Atkin and Bernard Darwin. She was the grand-daughter of Laurence and Mary Anne Ruck, the latter a descendant of a distinguished Welsh family with an estate outside Machynlleth. She wrote more than 100 romantic novels and led a life of adventure. She married another prolific author, **Oliver Onions**. She returned to Wales in 1939 and lived for the rest of her life at Pomona on Bodfor Terrace, and finally at the Bryntegwel care home, swimming daily until well into her 80s and being a conspicuous local figure.

Craig y don, oil painting, unknown artist.

Mid nineteenth century, before a large extension to the left by Lord Atkin, and the railway in front.

On the right is Craig y Don, the earliest house, being neo-Gothic and with decorative bargeboards. Originally more impressively set with views to the sea, it was the home of Lord Atkin of Aberdovey. It was extended by Lord Atkin, with substantial gardens and tennis courts above.

Just beyond Craig y Don is the site of the Corbet Arms, an early attempt to capture the tourist trade. Athelstan Corbet built the hotel on Ynys y Maengwyn land at the western end of Aberdyfi in 1829 to cater to the needs of an increasing number of visitors after the completion of the turnpike.

Further building began on the hillside of Penrhos, an area separated from the original settlement of Aberdyfi by a north-south rock ridge, cut through at the south end by the railway. At the north end the ridge was crossed in the early twentieth century by Gwelfor Road, leading east from Maes y Newydd. After Gwelfor Terrace, a survivor from earlier traditional development, **Gwelfor Road** is characterized by a mixture of styles, including a number of early tile-hung houses. They are not shown on the Ordnance Survey map of 1902, but must have been built soon after. Among a stylistic melting pot which includes modern infill, some houses on or near Gwelfor Road stand out. Most were designed by Charles F. Ellis:

Craig y Don, John Thomas, *c.*1890.

The house as extended by Lord Atkin and before recent alterations and planting between the road and railway.

- Garreg Wen and Nythfa (a pair of semi-detached bungalows), Charles F. Ellis.
- Gorwel, utterly charming with playful Arts and Crafts asymmetry. The detail slabs and the vernacular garden walls and round gate pillars are significant.
- Bryngolau, Charles F. Ellis.
- Monkshill, Corbett Lane, designed by Charles F. Ellis for Dr Jackson who had consulting rooms there.
- Dovey Heights, modernist, at the junction with Corbett Lane.
- Hendre (1910), perched on the rock above Craig y Don. Very imaginative Arts and Crafts, all shapes and angles.
- Glaslyn (1914), F. Howarth, of Tywyn.

Rhoslan is a long row of houses on a level terrace to the east, with their own access from the A496. The first houses are early twentieth-century, and include Murmur y Don, which is highly picturesque and very charming with a veranda and an irregular roof with slightly upturned eaves. The remainder of the row are varied and altered later detached houses. In the latter twentieth century development also spread into the former quarry.

Lord Atkin of Aberdovey

James (known as Dick) Atkin, a grandson of **Mary Anne** and **Laurence Ruck** of Pantlludw, outside Machynlleth, was born in Australia, but on the early death of his father returned to his grandmother's home. He was intensely proud of his Welshness and became much involved and highly respected locally. He became a Lord Justice of Appeal and Lord Atkin of Aberdovey in 1919.

He was a churchgoer and also a keen sportsman, playing golf with his relative, the outstanding golf writer **Bernard Darwin**. He is famous among lawyers. His leading judgment, in a case concerning the alleged unfortunate effects of an alleged snail in a bottle of ginger beer served in a café in Paisley, established the modern law of negligence. A dissenting judgment in 1941, defending individual liberty against the broad powers of the executive, was a landmark in law concerning the relationship between the courts and the State in times of national emergency.

The Corbet Arms Family Hotel and Post House, engraving, *c.*1850.

The hotel was originally at the edge of the sea, with a bowling green in front and bathing huts and donkey rides on the beach. It was rebuilt by the railway engineer Thomas Savin in 1867, with the hope of capitalising on visitors brought in by the railway. However, like his hotels at Borth and Aberystwyth, it struggled to survive, and was destroyed by fire in 1914. The empty shell was cleared away in 1968 to make way for a new primary school. That closed in 2013, and has been replaced by housing.

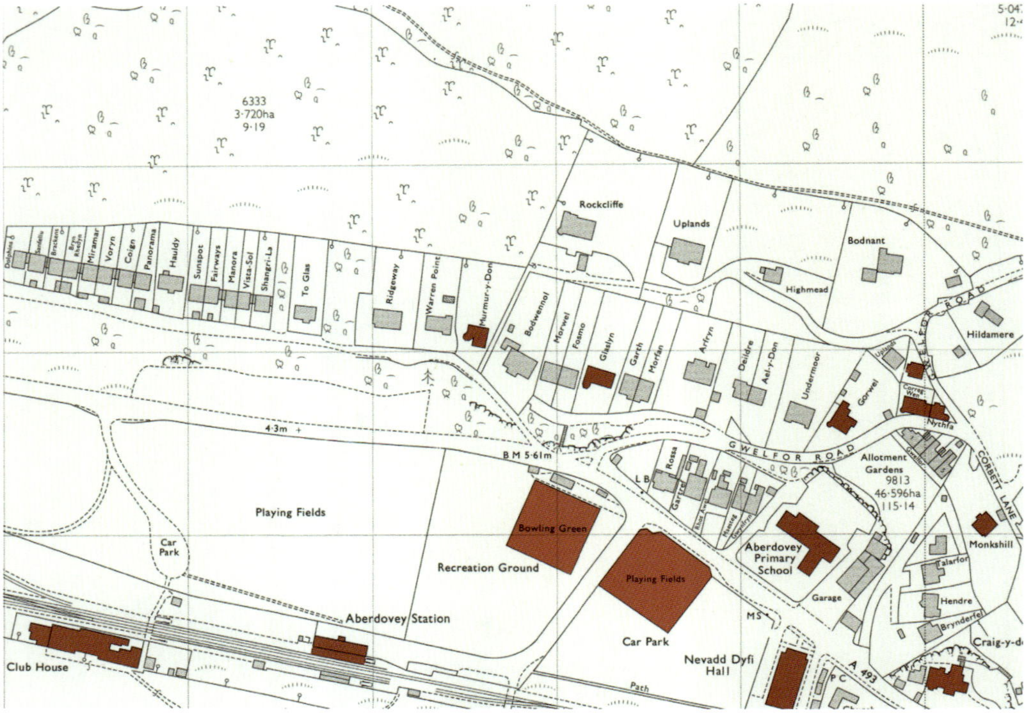

Ordnance Survey, 1: 2500, 1974.

Section to show the Gwelfor Road area. Buildings mentioned in the text are coloured red.

An area below Rhoslan, alongside the golf course and road, is common land known as Morfa Gypsies from the time it was used by itinerant gypsies.

At sea level, behind the sand dunes, drainage and the railway embankment enabled the creation of sports grounds and public buildings. More recent twentieth-century demand for housing and holiday homes has led to a sprawl of developments on both sides of the road.

On the estuary side of the road, the first building opposite Craig y Don was the Roman Catholic Church of Christ the King. Roman Catholics originally worshipped in the old Calvinistic Methodist chapel in Chapel Square, but in 1939 they were given a prefabricated garage brought in from Oswestry. A new church was built in 1974, but services ceased in 2015, and it was demolished and has been replaced by a private house.

Next door is **Neuadd Dyfi**, the very active village community centre built in 1957. Its predecessor, the Pavilion, was acquired from an army camp in Oswestry in 1920, and became a centre for village amateur dramatics, concerts and meetings.

Next door are the recreation ground and playing fields. The football pitch was established by the council in the early twentieth century. Aberdovey Bowling Club was founded in 1921, and now has a clubhouse with lawn bowls, tennis courts, putting green and a croquet

The golf course and clubhouse, with tents used by village boys on what is now the Penrhos Caravan Site, *c*.1900.

lawn. Beyond and south of the railway line is Penrhos Caravan Site, established in the 1940s on former common land that had previously been a popular camping ground.

Continuing along the main road, a left turn leads to the redbrick **railway station** (1872). Unfortunately, its canopy and associated workshops and stores were removed in the twentieth century and it is now a private house, and the station is unstaffed. Close by, on the sand dunes, is an intact Second World War pillbox, and on the seashore dry-stone walls which are the probable remains of two C-shaped fish traps.

Next is the entrance to the golf course. Established in 1892, Aberdyfi is one of the oldest golf clubs in Wales, the birthplace of the Welsh Golfing Union, and ranked high among British courses. It has been much loved by many descendants of founder members, including the Rucks, the Howells (Plas Penhelig), the Cave family of Trefeddian Hotel, and by other regular players. It was also a place for enterprising young caddies, who would gather on a sand dune with a good view of the blind No. 3 hole, and sing out the results of each shot in harmony: 'To the right', 'To the left' or a deep mournful 'In the bunker'. A notable caddie was a daughter of the Secretary. Once, when very tiny, her patron decided she was too small for the job and relieved her of the clubs after two holes. She trotted alongside, and on being given her wages asked: 'What time would you like me this afternoon?'

Golf clubhouses and view of Penrhos, c. 1900.

The original clubhouse of 1895 and attached artisans hut for non-members burnt down, and the present clubhouse was built in 1998. Three farms retain inherited grazing rights for cattle and sheep on the course, and there are paths to the sea beaches.

Trefeddian Hotel (named after a nearby farm), high on the hill, overlooks the golf course and the sea and has a great reputation among families and golfers. It was built in 1904 by Edward Morgan, local landowner and builder, and bought in 1907 by the Cave-Browne-Cave family who owned it until 2025. Its original decorative half timbering would have been more in place in a fashionable Normandy resort. Sadly, successive makeovers have sacrificed this delightful character for bulky, modern, but very comfortable blandness.

Just beyond the redbrick Trefeddian Hotel terrace, a tannery complex is seen to the right of the road on the Ordnance Survey first and second edition maps. The tanks were at the eastern edge, next to the stream. The site has now been redeveloped with housing.

A path on the seaward side leads to the site of the 1868 gas works which received gas in underground pipes from Tywyn Gas Works for storage in three gas holders. Now demolished, it has, since 2015, been a nature reserve owned by the community council.

Aberdyfi cemetery dates from 1885. There is melancholy evidence in the inscriptions on gravestones in churchyards and cemeteries of the many shipwrecks and drownings in the storms and treacherous currents around the bar, and also out in Cardigan Bay.

Bernard Darwin

Bernard Darwin (1876–1961) was a highly capable amateur golfer and the most famous of golf writers as the golf correspondent for *The Times* and an author of many books. He was the son of **Amy Ruck**, who died four days after his birth, and of Frank Darwin (the botanist **Sir Francis Darwin**) and was the grandson of **Charles** and **Emma Darwin** in whose home he grew up. He was a frequent visitor to his Welsh grandmother, **Mary Anne Ruck**, at Pantlludw, Machynlleth. A fine golfer, he wrote that, 'Aberdovey is the course my soul loves the best of all the courses in the world.' Among many distinguished relatives were his cousins and Aberdyfi residents, **Berta Ruck** and **Lord Atkin**.

Aberdyfi from the west, © Glyn Davies.

Trefeddian Hotel from the golf links, early twentieth century.

View from a Trefeddian Hotel bedroom.

The roadside car park is popular with those who cross the golf course to bathe on Cemetery Beach.

Further still, and hidden away from the road at the edge of the parish, Rhowniar is a particularly good Georgian Arts and Crafts house (1911–12). Designed by the prominent architect Oswald Milne, who briefly worked in Lutyens' office, it was built for William Kettle, replacing one built by his father, a very successful Midlands barrister. For a short while it was a girls' Outward Bound centre. It has the remains of a contemporary country house garden.

On the long Rhowniar drive is Cruck Hall, an unusually large, early sixteenth-century hall house with an impressive internal chimney. Almost certainly the oldest house in Aberdyfi, it is also the only building listed as II*.

Longer walks

There are numerous booklets, information sheets and maps which have details of many walks around Aberdyfi and further afield. Walks that can be combined in interesting ways not only have wonderful views but reveal a landscape of natural history, ancient place-names, early farmhouses and archaeological sites.

Afterword

The idea of this book came after many years of watching the Dyfi estuary's tide and weather, and of writing about the estuary. Research has been a revelation about places that I believed I knew well. Even so, it is no more than an introduction and there is more that can be found in the sources listed in 'How to find out more' on the following page. Even more remains to be discovered from archaeology, research on primary sources in libraries and archives, and from local observation and memories.

One of the greatest rewards has been the opportunity to meet and to talk with so many interesting, generous and knowledgeable people. Many have talked at length, exchanged emails, given much practical help and read drafts. Doris O'Keefe stimulated me to write about Aberdyfi, and has shown me documents and told me about her family history and made introductions. Libby Andrews has given invaluable advice and information throughout and organised introductions. She has also transformed my pages on natural history. Judith Alfrey, an architectural historian, has, with her husband Iain, walked me around the village and then read, corrected and added to the descriptions of buildings. Dai and Helen Williams have been generous with advice and images from their incomparable collection. Glyn Davies has been informative and provided remarkable aerial images taken from his microlight. David Roberts, Paul Fowles, David and Gay Richardson, Megan and John Reynolds and David Williams have been invaluable informants. Liz Fenwick drew informative and engaging maps. Eirian Jones at the supportive Y Lolfa has been a scrupulous copy editor. My designer, Jeremy Morgan of Fizog Design, has patiently and creatively transformed my material into a handsome book.

How to find out more

Local histories

D.W. Morgan (1877–1957), *Brief Glory* (Brython Press, 1949).
Son of Captain James Morgan, with many village relatives.

Lloyd, Lewis (1939–1997, *A Real Little Seaport: The port of Aberdyfi and its people, 1565–1920, Volume I.*
A meticulous scholar who devoted his life to the history of Meirionnydd.

Hugh Lewis, numerous booklets of Aberdyfi history and photographs. A member of a prominent village family who lived in Cliffside all his life and was much involved in village affairs.

Bernard Darwin (1876–1961), the best-known golf journalist and author who wrote much about his love for the Aberdyfi course founded by his family.

Richard Mayou, *The Dyfi Estuary: An Illustrated History* (Machynlleth Tabernacle Trust, 2021).

General Welsh histories and guides

Pevsner Architectural Guides: Buildings of Wales, Gwynedd (Yale University Press, 2009).

Redknap, Mark, Rees, Sian and Aberg, Alan (eds), *Wales and the Sea – 10,000 years of Welsh Maritime History* (RCHAMW, 2019).

Jenkins, Simon, *Wales: Churches, Houses, Castles* (Allen Lane, 2011).

Davies, R.R., *Owain Glyn Dŵr: Prince of Wales* (Y Lolfa, 2011).

Oxford History of Wales Series (Oxford University Press).
An outstanding and authoritative series by distinguished Welsh historians.

Websites

The web is a rich source of information. I have found the following particularly valuable:

Conservation Area Appraisal: Aberdyfi, Gwynedd. Report 2155 (2011).

Chambers Conservation Ltd, Aberdyfi. Conservation Area Appraisal and Management plan (2021).

Aberdovey Londoner www.aberdoveylondoner.com is highly recommended, entertaining and well-illustrated, but now no longer an active blog. It includes an excellent heritage section with scholarly referenced pieces on many of the topics referred to in this book.

The Royal Commission on the Ancient and Historical Monuments of Wales, an online catalogue of archaeology, buildings, industrial and maritime heritage. See (Coflein) www.coflein.gov.uk

Illustrations

I am grateful to the following for permission to use the images on the pages listed below:

Aberdyfi Literary Institute: 61, 86.
Libby Andrews: 103.
Glyn Davies: Front cover, 8, 13, 14, 17, 57, 99, 109.
Roy Fellows: 39, 92.
Liz Fenwick: 6, 11, 16, 59, 62
Simon Jenkins: 87.
Richard Mayou: 2, 15, 21, 32, 36, 40, 42, 56, 110.
Meirionnydd Record Office: 34, 51, 98.
National Library of Scotland (Ordnance Survey): 39, 52, 96, 106.
The National Library of Wales: 28, 33, 36, 42, 44, 45, 47, 50, 51, 63, 64, 65, 67, 70, 71, 72, 77, 79, 81, 82, 83, 89, 91, 93, 101, 104, 105, 107.
David Roberts: 48.
The Royal Commission on the Ancient and Historical Monuments of Wales: 7, 23, 41, 69, 94.
Nicola and Adam Ruck: 53.
School of Art, Aberystwyth University: 78.
Mary Warrell: End paper.
Dai and Helen Williams: 38, 43, 74, 90, 108, 110.

About the author

Richard Mayou was Professor of Psychiatry at Oxford University and Fellow of Nuffield College and is now retired. He has visited the Dyfi area every year of his life, since 1952 staying at a family house on the very edge of the estuary between Aberdyfi and Pennal. The photograph shows him and his late wife, Ann, on the hillside above Cwm Maethlon, close to Eglwys Gwyddelod, in 2011.